Praise for *U.N. Agenda 21: Environmental Piracy*

Dr. Johnson, who survived childhood in Communist Romania, is one of the most prominent voices of her day on Agenda 21. An in-demand public speaker, popular radio show guest and prolific columnist, Dr. Johnson cuts through U.N. confusing rhetoric and doublespeak, laying bare for readers the terrible toll of Agenda 21 on sovereignty and freedom.

Only an author with first-hand experience under Communist rule could have recognized that Agenda 21 bears the same imprimatur as Communism and explain in gripping detail which forms Agenda 21 is taking in your hometown.

Written in language any lay person can understand, Dr. Ileana Johnson's *U.N. Agenda 21: Environmental Piracy* just as easily could have been titled, *Agenda 21 Made Easy*.
-   Judi McLeod, Editor, Canada Free Press

If you are looking for an entertaining, thrilling or even a pontificating book, this is not for you. However, if the goal is to learn about and do something about the most insidious, persistent and deadly threat to human liberty, Dr. Ileana Johnson Paugh is the authority to look up to because of her special expertise in the subject of this work and her unique perspective, having lived half her life in a communist nation and the rest in the U.S.A. We are indisputably on the road to serfdom. If we are to return to being sovereigns as God intended and as the Founding Fathers designed into our precious Constitution, new intellectual giants will have to emerge. Ileana is one of them.
-   Jatinder Singh Mann, M.D.

Other Books by Dr. Ileana Johnson Paugh

Echoes of Communism
Lessons From An American by Choice

Liberty on Life Support
Essays on American Exceptionalism, Immigration, Education, and Economy

U.N. Agenda 21: Environmental Piracy

Dr. Ileana Johnson Paugh

ISBN: 0615716474
ISBN-13: 978-0615716473

DEDICATION

I dedicate this book to my patient husband David who is a constant source of strength, love, patience, and computer expertise. He is my enabler, the one person who is always by my side with words of encouragement.

Contents

ACKNOWLEDGEMENTS

I am indebted to my husband David who is my research enabler. When I am discouraged, he is my number one cheerleader. His patience and calm demeanor diffuse any temporary impatience.

I owe a debt of gratitude to my tough Language and Literature teacher in high school who gave me a solid grasp and understanding of grammar and syntax. I did not fully appreciate her teaching mastery at the time and her toughness frustrated me at times.

I would like to tell my high school English teacher that I have regretted often my stubbornness in her class – I told her repeatedly that I resentfully took English for two years, a language that I would never use. I was obviously wrong.

To my Home Economics teacher, Mrs. Enescu, who is 94 years old now and just as sharp as ever, I would like to tell that I have used the sewing skills she taught me many times over the years, yet I was never a very appreciative student during our four hours a week class. Sitting still for that long was quite challenging to me.

To my friend Sevil Kalayci, thank you for believing that my writing is worth sharing and encouraging me to send it for publication.

To Dana Malisca, my constant friend of twelve years, first grade through twelfth, with whom I recently reunited in Romania after a lifetime, thank you for our heated daily debates that turned both of us into the fantastic teachers that we are today. Dana is a Geography teacher at the same high school we graduated from years ago. I ran into her in the faculty lounge when I was visiting the newly renovated high school.

I could not be who I am today without the constant love and support of my parents who always believed that education is the key to success and have taught me early on to be independent and to follow my dreams even if that means immigrating to the best country in the world, the United States of America. As a parent, I now understand their sacrifice and how hard it was for my parents to let go of their only child who crossed an ocean to find opportunity and freedom.

Preface

I am not sure when subsequent generations, our children, grandchildren, and great-grandchildren will no longer be permitted access in zones marked off-limits to human habitation and trespassing in accordance with the dictates of UN Agenda 21 and the now infamous Wildlands Project map.

The map was produced by Dr. Michael Coffman, editor of *Discerning the Times Digest and NewsBytes* and CEO of *Sovereignty International*, to stop the ratification of the international treaty on Convention on Biological Diversity one hour before the scheduled cloture and ratification vote. (Congressional Record S13790)

The mandate of the Convention of Biological Diversity draws buffer zones, core reserves and corridors to protect biodiversity. Areas in green will allow housing. Areas in yellow will be buffer zones, highly regulated with no homes and possible hiking. Red areas will be core reserves and corridors off-limits to human access and human habitation. There is already limited use of red areas via no management or resource harvesting through Wilderness, Critical Habitat, and Roadless Areas.

Dr. Coffman's map also includes the Border 21/La Paz Sidebar Agreement of NAFTA, 120 mile wide international zone of cooperation, and Indian and military reservations.

The idea of a One World Government/Order and Agenda 21 has been around since the turn of the 20th century. To see written evidence, just look on the back of a one-dollar bill. Featured prominently under the Masonic pyramid are the Latin words, *Novus Ordo Seclorum*, the New World Order.

It was not until 1992, after numerous United Nations conferences around the globe spanning decades and a concerted effort by third world governments led by individuals like Maurice Strong and Gro Harlem Brundtland that the UN Agenda 21 became reality at the UN Conference on Environment and Development (UNCED) in 1992 in Rio de Janeiro, Brazil.

This conference produced three documents: The United Nations Framework Convention on Climate Change (an international treaty), the United Nations Convention on Biological Diversity (an international treaty), and UN Agenda 21 (not a treaty but a "soft law").

President Herbert Walker Bush signed along with 178 countries but refused to sign the United Nations Convention on Biological Diversity because it required transfer of technology without recognition of proprietary rights. However, President Bush said, "It is the sacred principles enshrined in the UN Charter to which the American people will henceforth pledge their allegiance." I am sure the American people were very surprised or perhaps totally unaware that a U.S. President would pledge allegiance to a foreign body instead of the U.S. Constitution.

UN Agenda 21 is a "soft law" document, not ratified by Congress. Parts of it have been incorporated into other laws passed because Congressmen do not read the bills they pass or do not understand the full scope of the UN Agenda 21. The 40 chapter document limits the behavior and freedoms of individuals and firms, involving every facet of human life.

A video dated October 2, 1992 and taken from C-SPAN archives shows discussions on the House floor about Agenda 21 in which both Democrats and Republicans are in favor of conforming fully to the recommendations of UN Agenda 21 in spite of the oath they took to defend the U.S. Constitution and the sovereignty of our country. A much younger and stuttering Nancy Pelosi introduced a bill to follow the 1992 Rio Earth Summit to conform to UN Agenda 21, its local sustainable community practices, and to follow international law. (http://www.youtube.com/watch?feature=player_embedded&v=XU BwIJWH7ew#)

UN Agenda 21 makes suggestions and recommendations that are adapted into law at the state and local levels through comprehensive land use plans which are voted on and included by the board of supervisors into local zoning codes. Citizens do not understand its damaging ramifications to their private property, the ability to make a living, to use their land, grow food in their gardens, sell their produce freely, and engage in agriculture. Local land owners do not have the opportunity to provide their input into the decision-making process, they are at the mercy of "visioning committees" and the board of supervisors, often plants or paid subscribers to the One World Government's UN Agenda 21 document.

UN Agenda 21 goals include but are not limited to:
- Redistribution of population according to resources
- Government control of land use in order to achieve equitable distribution of resources
- Land use control through zoning and planning
- Government control of excessive profits from land use
- Urban and rural land control through public land ownership
- Developing rights must be held by public authorities via "regionalist" authorities

President Bill Clinton facilitated President Herbert Walker Bush's initial commitment by signing an executive order which created the President's Council on Sustainable Development to translate UN Agenda 21 into U.S. public policy under the guise of eco-system management.

One World Governance in the name of protecting the environment, racial justice, and social justice/equity is a communist system that redistributes wealth and promotes universal health care as a human right.

Harvey Rubin, the Vice Chair of ICLEI, proclaimed his vision of a communistic sustainable world in which "Individual rights must take a back seat to the collective."

One World Governance will control:
- Energy production, delivery, distribution, and consumption via Smart Grid, Smart Meters, and Renewable/Clean/Green resources
- Food growth and production via FDA regulations, and Codex Alimentarius
- Education control via a curriculum centered on environment and Mother Earth and global citizenship (i.e., No Child Left Inside Act in Maryland)

- Water through irrigation denial in agriculture, home use, recreation activities; destruction of dams and reservoirs; abolishing hydro-electric generation use of water as a contributor to the now discredited theory that greenhouse gases cause global warming
- Land control by abolishing private property
- Finances (one world currency to replace the U.S. dollar as the world's reserve currency)
- De-population (restructuring the family unit and reducing population to "manageable levels" through sterilization and eugenics)
- No borders/no sovereignty
- No national language and culture (a multi-cultural mélange devoid of a nation's history, and shameless promotion of global citizenship)
- Mobility restriction to 5 minute-walk/bike from work, school, shopping
- Longer distance travel through rail use
- Homestead by stacking people in high-rise tenements in order to designate formerly privately-owned land for wildlife habitat

The One World Governance of the UN Agenda 21 requires that every societal decision be based on the environmental impact on global land use, global education, and global population control and reduction. They have deemed "not sustainable" most human activities that form our modern civilization: private property, fossil fuels, consumerism, farming, irrigation, commercial agriculture, pesticides, herbicides, farmlands, grazing of livestock, paved roads, golf courses, ski lodges, logging, dams, reservoirs, fences, power lines, suburban living, and the family unit.

"Current lifestyles and consumption patterns of the affluent middle class – involving high meat intake, use of fossil fuels, appliances, home and work air conditioning, and suburban housing are not sustainable." (Maurice Strong, Secretary General of the UN's Earth Summit, 1992)

"We must make this place an insecure and inhospitable place for Capitalists and their projects – we must reclaim the roads and plowed lands, halt dam construction, tear down existing dams, free shackled rivers and return to wilderness millions of tens of millions of acres of presently settled land." (Dave Foreman, Earth First)

Public Private Partnerships and ICLEI have enabled the spread and encroachment of UN Agenda 21. Public Private Partnerships, programs between the federal government and non-governmental organizations (NGOs), have implemented with tax dollars Sustainable Development policies at the local level such as Smart Growth, Green Growth, Green Building Codes, Going Green, and many others.

The International Council for Local Environmental Initiatives (ICLEI) now called Local Governments for Sustainability has channeled grants with the help of the American Planning Association to the municipalities around the country. These grants were badly needed by struggling communities and came with strings attached such as "visioning consensus," the vision of a third, unelected government tier coming from the United Nations and non-profit foundations who promote the interest of wild animals over those of humans.

There is never a shortage of new converts – the educational system is deliberately dumbing down our students in order to accept the Sustainable Development goals. "Generally, more highly educated people, who have higher incomes, consume more resources than poorly educated people, who tend to have lower incomes. In this case, more education increases the threat to sustainability."

In some states, the curriculum includes "constructivism," a teaching method by which "students construct [their own] understandings of reality and [realize] that objective reality is not knowable."

"The aim of education is the knowledge not of facts but of values." Whose values will educate our children? Will it be the atheist, Gaia-centric values of government indoctrination?

The New World Order teachers recommend Connected Mathematics because "Mathematics is man-made, is arbitrary, and good solutions are arrived at by **consensus** among those who are considered expert." With the right consensus of experts, two plus two may not be four but five.

"The curriculum does not emphasize arithmetic and some students may not do well on tests assessing computational skills... We believe such a trade-off in favor of Connected Mathematics is very much to students' advantage in... the world of work."

According to Henry Lamb, UNESCO, another tentacle of the United Nations, had taught seminars to teachers and disseminated curriculum materials that promoted the idea that nationalism was bad and had to be replaced with global citizenship. The textbooks of the International Baccalaureate plant the seeds of prejudice against national pride and support the idea that world/global citizenship and world governance are viable solutions to the future of a socially, racially, and economically unjust planet.

As I described in my essays the countless places where I had encountered Sustainable Development, I came to the realization that, because United Nations Agenda 21 is so insidious and so much part of every facet of our society, it will take a miracle to dismantle it.

Regulating Us Into Economic Destruction

In accordance with the law, the Executive Branch must document annually the number of new regulatory actions it plans for each coming year. The Administration's regulatory agenda in 2011 had 4,257 new regulatory actions. At least 219 had an economic impact of $100 million or more. That was an increase of nearly 15 percent over the previous year when it had 191. Americans were told by the Obama administration that some economically significant regulations will have economic impacts of tens of billions of dollars.

House Speaker John Boehner (R-OH) sent a letter on August 26, 2011, to President Obama, asking the White House to provide Congress with a list of all regulatory actions that would have an economic impact of $1 billion or more. Boehner sent a similar request for information on August 16, 2010 when he was the House Republican leader. The requested data was never provided.

Dudley said in Politico, "Some activity is required by new legislative mandates – particularly Dodd-Frank Wall Street Reform/Consumer Protection Act and Obamacare. Others, including EPA's regulation of greenhouse gases under the Clean Air Act, are based on new judicial interpretation of statutes passed 20 or more years ago – and do not necessarily reflect the priorities of any recent Congress. But some are discretionary actions, like EPA's pending decision to tighten ozone standards. That is likely to slow economic growth in thousands of counties across the nation and impose costs of $20 billion to $90 billion per year, according to the agency's own estimates."

Regulations are enacted every day by fiat by the current administration and its various governmental agencies with or without congressional approval at such a dizzying speed that Americans no longer have the capacity to keep up with the sheer volume and correctly assess the negative impact that they have short-term or long-term on the U.S. economy, our sovereignty, private property, and our freedom.

Global warming, climate change, carbon credits, environmental sustainability, smart growth, smart grid, smart meters, sustainable communities, all United Nations Agenda 21-driven initiatives are being forced on all communities across the country at the local, state, and government level. There are no agencies left that have not yet adopted some sustainable plans.

Flying in the face of our Constitution that protects private property, United Nations Agenda 21 believes in government control of our economy, environment, and social equity because "individual rights must take a back seat to the collective."

George Washington said, "Private property and freedom are inseparable." John Adams agreed that "Property must be secured, or liberty cannot exist." How much clearer can we state our collective desires to be free? We do not wish to be slaves to the United Nations; we are an independent Constitutional Republic.

The UN General Assembly President, Joseph Deiss, does not understand our wishes to remain independent because he stated on August 10, 2011, speaking in Chile, that the UN must be reformed in order to "claim its rightful role in achieving more effective global governance in the 21st century." Mr. Deiss underlined "the UN's essential role as the unique umbrella for the whole system of **global governance** due to its universality, unique legitimacy and its value-based nature." As a free American citizen, I am opposed to UN's values of abolishing private property and installation of collectivization under global government control.

Yet on September 22, 2010, the President signed a "Presidential Policy Directive on Global Development," the first of its kind by a U.S. administration. This is a policy focused on "sustainable development outcomes," the hallmark of United Nation's Agenda 21.

The directive is to "use U.S. leadership in the multilateral development banks, U.N. agencies, other international organizations, other donors, foundations, nongovernmental organizations, the private sector, and other stakeholders to deploy the full range of our development tools and policies at our disposal." We are to "place greater emphasis on building **sustainable capacity** in the public sectors of our partners and at their national and community levels to provide basic services over the long-term. How about providing services to our bankrupted economy?

Because Congress does not agree to all of these United Nations schemes to steal our property and destroy our economy, they are being passed by fiat, executive orders, proclamations, directives, and generous grants given to local communities who are suffering under our depressed, mismanaged economy.

The latest example of collaborative effort to "invest" (read "force") in **sustainable communities** was announced on August 17, 2011 between HUD and EPA and involved $5.65 million grant "competitively awarded to eight organizations." Each grantee was uniquely qualified to "build the capacity of sustainable communities in six outcome areas."

The Institute for Sustainable Communities from Montpelier, VT will "create a National Sustainability Learning Network."

The University of Louisville Research Foundation, Inc. from Louisville, KY will "address the need for incorporating water, infrastructure planning and investments with other planning efforts."

The Coalition of Utah's Future/Project 2000 from Salt Lake City, UT will "work to build skills in Scenario Planning techniques and tools."

Reconnecting America in Washington, D.C. will "develop effective implementation strategies for economic development and local and regional plans."

Policy Link in Oakland, Ca and Place Matters, Inc. in Denver, CO will "work with communities to advance **social equity** in planning, participation, and decision making."

The NADO Research Foundation in Washington, D.C. and the Minnesota Housing Partnership in St. Paul, MN will "target their efforts in strengthening sustainability practices for tribes, small towns, and rural places."

Having seen such plans in action under communism, when they confiscated our land, property and money in the name of collectivization, and researching UN Agenda 21, I can recognize its nefarious goals and plans. I wish other Americans could see that these Orwellian, euphemistically named programs and grants are nothing but economic shakedowns, aimed at destroying our freedom and turning us into a "fundamentally changed" America, a change that most Americans do not embrace.

Smart Growth America!

A robocall from the Magisterial District Supervisor and "all his Smart Growth friends" invited me not long ago to a tour of Belmont Bay, a mixed-used residential area with a new George Mason University environmental science facility. The call came to the right person but for the wrong reasons.

The on-line brochure of Belmont Bay sounded wonderful, golf club, walking paths, a marina, shops, who would not want their neighborhood to have amenities that make life so much easier, especially in the context of northern Virginia, which is one of the most traffic-congested areas in the country, with the largest population growth of 40 percent. (Census Bureau, 2012)

The words he used, Smart Growth, flagged my attention immediately, since I recognized one of the euphemisms used by UN Agenda 21 to hide land use control, regulation, and confiscation under the guise of environmental protection.

As my writing was informing other people of the dangers of the UN Agenda 21 and ICLEI (International Council for Local Environmental Initiatives) across the country, the Green Environmental Monster was lurking in my very own back yard. In April 2011, our supervisor had sponsored a Smart Growth Symposium for all "residents, business leaders, and property owners." I am a property owner and never heard of this symposium and neither did all others whom I asked.

Among the three speakers, Richard B. Norment, the Executive Director of the National Council for Public-Private Partnerships stood out as the conduit for UN Agenda 21 goals, along with a local banker and a lawyer.

The document presented indicated that Community Development Authorities were "created by governing body upon petition of 51 percent of landowners by area or assessed value." None of the landowners I asked heard of such an authority or petition.

Mecklenburg County, NC was used as an example of a successful mixed-use development, "transit-oriented" and "town center" focused. A light rail line was projected to parallel the relocated freight line.

The presenter from the National Council for Public-Private Partnerships emphasized the **Stakeholder Support**, a key element of the infiltration of UN Agenda 21 into our communities through various NGOs (non-governmental organizations).

My discovery came on the heels of Senator Robert Menendez (D) introduction of SB 1621, **Livable Communities Act** on September 22, 2011 with 17 Democrat cosponsors. If the bill would pass, it would create an Office of Sustainable Housing and Communities at the U.S. Department of Housing and Urban Development (HUD), more bureaucracy to control our private land and housing by government fiat. As of now, the bill is still in committee.

The media made no report of this bill as they were too preoccupied with the regime's latest diversion tactic - the paid Marxist global warming lunatic collegiate fringe, the Wall Street Occupiers, "arrogantly stupid and smug," as a famous talk show host described them, protesting capitalism and Wall Street in various venues across the country, while asking for entitlements the rest of us must provide. Being the useful communist idiots that they are, it had not crossed their minds to protest the colleges that charge the outrageous tuitions while sitting on millions and billions of dollars in endowments and paying college professors handsomely to indoctrinate them into communism and anti-Americanism.

"The Office of Sustainable Housing and Communities at HUD would coordinate federal policies that foster **Sustainable Development**, Healthy Homes, and administer HUD's

Sustainability Initiatives. This office would also award **Comprehensive Planning** grants, **Community Challenge** grants, and encourage transit-oriented development."

All elements in this bill that I highlighted are further implementation of United Nation's Agenda 21 goals by federal government awarding grants to communities, forcing federal policy on states and exacerbating their financial needs when the grants expire.

Smart Growth America is another NGO (non-government organization) that pushes ICLEI's goals, as their site states, "Smart Growth is a better way to build our urban, suburban, and rural communities." They are concerned with our transportation, our communities, and reducing carbon emissions. They are using "**steering committees**" and "**visioning**" to change our lives in accordance with the United Nation's vision of a one world government controlled by a few. Under the guise of saving the planet from the destructive humans, private property must be abolished; everybody must live in mixed-use zones, five-minute walk from work and school, moving about on public buses or light rail. Land must be given back to its intended wilderness.

In spite of evidence to the contrary that global warming is man-made, progressives are marching on, trying to reshape, restructure, control, and fundamentally change the way we live, according to their dictates and twisted vision of the world.

Smart Growth America is offering free technical assistance to communities "interested in smart growth strategies." Although most Americans create their own dreams of prosperity and happiness, progressives are saying, "To understand the new American dream, we have to understand the new America."

RailVolution, a four-day conference in D.C., discussed "strategies for building livable communities served by transit." The conference was opened by the president of an NGO called LOCUS, with a speech on "Responsible Real Estate Developers and Investors." Manuel Pastor, a Professor of American Studies and Ethnicity at the University of Southern California, Los Angeles, joined in the opening conference. If you wonder what ethnicity and American Studies of Ethnicity have to do with transit and American communities, you are not alone.

Pastor emphasized **walkable** neighborhoods because the U.S. is diversifying ethnically and racially, and growing older. Is that a good reason to move masses of people in high-rise tenements with high population concentration? Because we are more racially and ethnically diverse we must live in high-rise, concentrated areas? Seniors have done quite well in single-family homes and, when polled, they prefer to live independently.

Americans must wake up fast to this "green" invasion in our way of life: smart green growth, green transportation, saving the green planet, sustainable development, sustainable agriculture, and sustainable green jobs. Everything now is **sustainable** and all jobs and activities are **green**.

There is no green industry. We have windmills and we build solar panels expensively. Wind and solar power cannot provide enough electricity for our huge economy. Nobody has built a nuclear power plant since the seventies. There are no green jobs. There are traditional jobs, which have been given the euphemistic name of "green." It is environmental piracy plain and simple.

Beware of the Green Environmental Monster coming to your community, the excuse for United Nations to take over our economy, take over private property, and set the country back a few decades to the level of third world countries in the name of "social justice." Watch for these signs and language of UN Agenda 21 activities underway in your town:

- Installation of Smart Meters in your area, an illegal surveillance device without a warrant in the name of reducing electricity consumption and costs by cutting your power at peak usage and causing all sorts of health ailments because of radiation from the meter itself
- Your area is a member of ICLEI (International Council for Local Environmental Initiatives) or ICMA (International City/County Management Association)
- Your area has a Vision, Master, or Comprehensive Plan that has been adopted in the last 5-10 years, promoting the "Triple Bottom Line," or the three Es of Sustainable Development (Environment, Economy, and Social Equity)
- Your community supports Smart Growth, New Urbanism, and Resilient Communities with emphasis on using light rail, bike paths, walking, public transportation, discouraging the use of cars.

- Some communities narrow the roads to make them less accessible or install thousands of speed bumps; parking is at a premium and no parking garages are planned.
- Sustainable agriculture and community gardens are emphasized, encouraging a shift away from traditional free market driven food system, providing food just for the local community
- Your city established an Urban Growth Boundary – anything beyond it is considered "sprawl" and "blight." It is discouraged through incentives and regulations.
- Your town has joined Public-Private Partnerships, local regional councils, state, or federal government to promote Sustainable Communities Planning or Initiatives.
- Measurement of wealth through GDP (Gross Domestic Product) is discouraged while "happiness" and "well-being" become measures of wealth.
- A "New American Dream" is advertised as "living simply."
- Green energy, wind and solar, are most important, fossil fuels are evil.
- More and more restrictions and regulations are placed on land use, farm, residential, and commercial, in order to preserve the wilderness, small creatures, and natural resources at the expense of humans.
- The community is buying more and more "green space" and returning it to wilderness.
- You find a chart in your local government's documents with three concentric circles with the words, Environment, Economy, Equity written in the middle of each circle.
- Community leaders subscribe to global warming as a manmade fact. They take action to lower the community's carbon footprint by adopting "green" LEED building and energy code standards for construction and development, including incentives, benchmarks, and retrofitting.
- Your town belongs to Earth Charter, the Sierra Club's Cool Cities Initiative, the Audubon Society's Sustainable Community Initiative, or your mayor has signed the U.S. Conference of Mayors' Climate Protection Agreement.
- Officials refer to your town as a "transition town," a "resilient city," or a "livable community" and begin teaching "globalism," "interdependence with nature," and "interconnectedness."

- Social Equity vocabulary is being used in your community such as "food justice," "economic and environmental justice," "fairness," "direct democracy," "diversity," "food deserts," "social justice," and "wealth redistribution."
- NGOs (non-governmental organizations) become involved in your city's planning through other "stakeholders" in the "collaborative, consensus-building," "visioning" process that takes about 18 months to complete and details your community's future without input from the voters.
- Your school system starts teaching children how to be good "global citizens" and stewards of the environment via International Baccalaureate and other UN sponsored education agendas.
- Your local government authorities start to exceed their constitutionally granted powers by working with private international and national organizations through Public-Private Partnerships.
- You notice a significant push toward "social justice," interfaith initiatives that promote "one world" along with community diversity, multiculturalism, sameness of faiths, social inclusion, and environmental stewardship. (Darin Moser)

Can we stop the Green Monster of UN Agenda 21 before our country is "fundamentally transformed" as the President promised before his Inauguration? The United Nations' assault on our country began long before the American public became aware of its existence and of the negative effects on our country's economy and its sovereignty. Many Americans are still blissfully unaware. Few are taking the issue seriously. Could it be too late to reverse this social, moral, and economic destruction?

Sustainable Health: Forced into Health Prevention

I was greeted one day at the doctor's office by a full waiting room, reminiscent of communist polyclinics. It was almost three hours before I saw the doctor for less than five minutes. He was unfocused and hurried.

Six months ago, the wait would have been fifteen minutes and the doctor would have been relaxed, with plenty of time to spend with his patients. I asked him why such a long wait and hurry. He rolled his eyes and said, "New Obamacare regulations and compliance."

On June 10, 2010, the President signed an Executive Order creating the National Prevention, Health Promotion, and Public Health Council. The National Prevention Council, chaired by Surgeon General Regina Benjamin, was "charged with providing coordination and leadership at the federal level and among all executive departments and agencies with respect to prevention, wellness and health promotion practices."

With input from the "public and interested stakeholders, the National Prevention Council was charged with developing a **National Prevention Strategy**.

The **National Prevention Strategy** was released on June 16, 2011. The suggestions for this strategy came from "240 website

11

submissions and letters from dozen organizations (not named in the document) submitted directly to the National Prevention Council and the Office of the Surgeon General." The Surgeon General's website carried the proposal and the "discussion." No media devoted time and effort to this story. Yet 313 million Americans (give or take a few illegals) are now going to be subject to a strategy that was never put to a vote or referendum.

The National Prevention Strategy is a comprehensive plan that enforces good health not just from quality medical care, "but also from clean air and water, safe outdoor spaces for physical activity, safe worksites, healthy foods, violence-free environments and healthy homes. Prevention should be woven into all aspects of our lives, including where and how we live, learn, work, and play. Everyone – businesses, educators, health care institutions, government, communities and every single American – has a role in creating a healthier nation." If this sounds Orwellian, it is, but you have not heard the rest.

Did you think that Obama care and Agenda 21 were not interwoven? The word **"sustainable"** appeared at least a couple of times in the 125 page Summary of Obamacare.

The National Prevention Strategy is not just concerned with addressing the leading causes of death and disability in the United States (heart disease, cancer, stroke, chronic respiratory diseases, and unintentional injuries), but also with "preventable behaviors – including tobacco use, poor nutrition, physical activity, and excessive alcohol use." These priorities have to align with **Healthy People 2020** initiative:

- Eliminate health **disparities** (Euphemism for spreading the wealth)
- Promote healthy development and **healthy behaviors** across life stages (Who decides what is and is not healthy, sounds very controlling and totalitarian)
- Create social and physical environments that promote good health (Are we going to be moved to some Elysian Fields, the land of milk and honey?)
- Interventions will reach beyond the health care and public health sectors to include activities that influence health in areas such as:
  Housing
  Transportation

Food and nutrition
In-school and outdoor education
The workplace
The environment"

If this is not Orwellian enough, required by the Affordable Care Act, the President established an Advisory Group on January 26, 2011 when he appointed 13 people as members, adding two more members on April 8, 2011. Some of the members are doctors; however, the majority are bureaucrats. This advisory group gives guidance to members of the National Prevention Council.

There are 18 members of the National Prevention Council, an interesting mixture of non-medical bureaucrats, with the exception of two who are medical doctors.

- Surgeon General Regina Benjamin, Council Chair
- Secretary Kathleen Sebelius, Department of Health and Human Services
- Secretary Tom Vilsack, Department of Agriculture
- Secretary Arne Duncan, Department of Education
- Chairman Jon Leibowitz, Federal Trade Commission
- Secretary Hilda L. Solis, Department of Labor
- Secretary Janet A. Napolitano, Department of Homeland Security
- Administrator Lisa P. Jackson, Environmental Protection Agency
- Director R. Gil Kerlikowske, Office of National Drug Control Policy
- Director Melody Barnes, Domestic Policy Council
- Assistant Secretary-Indian Affairs Larry Echo Hawk, Department of the Interior
- Acting Chief Executive Officer Robert Velasco II, Corporation for National and Community Service
- Secretary Robert M. Gates, Department of Defense
- Secretary Shaun Donovan, Department of Housing and Urban Development
- Attorney General Eric H. Holder, Jr., Department of Justice
- Secretary Erik K. Shinseki, Department of Veteran Affairs
- Director Jacob J. Lew, Office of Management and Budget
- Secretary Ray LaHood, Department of Transportation

These individuals intend to promote for the rest of us, a **sustainable healthy lifestyle**. It is lofty to believe that people choose healthy lifestyles. Forcing people to live healthy in a manner that meets with the government's approval is an entirely different story. How is that the government's job to dictate how we live? How are they going to enforce this strategy in real life? How does a safe community and healthy **stakeholders** need the Department of Defense? How can you force reduction of preventable death, disease, and disability in the United States?

A program that mirrors Agenda 21 is the Department of Housing and Urban Development's **Partnership for Sustainable Communities** (part of National Prevention Strategy) which "helps improve access to affordable housing and transportation options and reduces transportation costs while protecting the environment in communities throughout the country. This partnership promotes **equitable development** to protect the environment, another code word for **re-distribution of wealth**, the Democrats' pet project. How is this related to our citizens' health? It seems to me that it aims to protect the environment at the expense of humans, one of the tenets of Agenda 21.

The Department of Housing and Urban Development also lists in the National Prevention Strategy, the **Green and Healthy Homes Initiative,** a "public-private partnership that implements a cost-effective and integrated approach to create energy-efficient and healthy housing through federal and philanthropic investments." What is healthy housing? Do we not have building codes in place and sanitation?

The most blatant UN Agenda 21 item of this National Prevention Strategy that has nothing to do with health is the Department of Interior's **America Great Outdoors Initiative,** which supports a "grassroots approach to protecting our lands and waters and connecting all Americans to their **natural and cultural heritage**.

The Bureau of Indian Affairs, within the Department of Interior, aims to develop the next generation of conservationists by targeting youth and encouraging outdoor activity." Yes, there are health benefits to being outdoors; I just do not understand how that is going to preserve **my** cultural heritage. It may preserve Indian heritage and push Mrs. Obama's **Let's Move** campaign as part of "prioritizing traditional native food that consists of locally grown, organic foods."

The Department of Transportation is pushing, as part of National Prevention Strategy, the **Safe Routes to School Program,** walking and bicycling to school. This program makes "walking and bicycling to school safer and more appealing transportation choices, thus encouraging a healthy and active lifestyle from an early age." More appealing transportation choices to whom? What if a child lives miles from school or in an unsafe or high-traffic area? What parent in his right mind would encourage a child to bike or walk at any age through heavy traffic and unsafe zones?

The **Neighborhood Revitalization Initiative** is another National Prevention Strategy goal that has "spreading the wealth" written all over it. The White House Domestic Policy Council, Department of Housing and Urban Development, Education, Justice, Health and Human Services, and Treasury are planning to transform, with massive infusion of cash, bad neighborhoods into places that provide opportunities, resources, and financial aid to people to "maximize their life outcomes, including achieving health."

We have been throwing billions of dollars at the "war on poverty" since its inception and we are currently losing this war. Throwing more money in the mix is not going to change the outcome. Changing welfare policy to encourage maintenance of the nucleus family (father, mother, child), instead of rewarding unwed mothers with more welfare, would go a long way to restore the health of our society.

Teaching children about our Judeo-Christian heritage in school, pride in history, pride in being American, and teaching right from wrong would also go a long way to restore health to our nation.

Taking freedoms away from the rest of us, and forcing citizens into a healthy lifestyle decided by all-knowing arrogant bureaucrats, who push servitude, UN Agenda 21, and environmental stewardship down our throats under the manufactured excuse of caring for our health, is Orwellian to say the least.

Welcome to UN Agenda 21's Walkability

HUD Secretary announced on July 28, 2011 the availability of $95 million to support **sustainable local initiatives** through the fiscal year 2011 Regional Planning and Community Challenge Planning Grant Programs. It seems like a good idea except that it is dedicated to **sustainable communities,** another pet word of United Nations Agenda 21. It is a good idea if you want to live in housing tenements with no cars while the streets are replaced by trains.

Regionalism or **regional planning** is also a bad idea because it introduces a new level of authority, superseding the local and metropolitan governments.

HUD's grant money places emphasis on land use, transportation, infrastructure with special priority on arts, culture, philanthropy, and innovative ideas. I had no idea that HUD's mission included arts and philanthropy.

HUD's Group 1 Funds "can be used to support the preparation of Regional Plans for **sustainable development.**

HUD's Group 2 Funds "can be used to support efforts to modify existing plans so that they are in accordance with the Partnership for Sustainable Communities' Six Livability Principles." Americans and Congress have not been asked to vote on these six livability principles.

1. Provide more transportation choices.
2. Promote equitable, affordable housing.
3. Enhance economic competitiveness.
4. Support existing communities.
5. Coordinate policies and leverage investment.
6. Value communities and neighborhoods.

President H.W. Bush signed in Rio, Brazil, United Nation's Agenda 21, binding us to third world dictatorships' agendas of impoverishing the United States and bringing it in line with the rest of the third world, erasing borders and our Constitution in the name of environmental protection, and taking private and productive farmland and returning it to wilderness.

The Community Challenge Planning grant program "will be competitively awarded to state, local and tribal governments for efforts such as **amending or replacing local master plans, zoning and building codes to promote mixed-use development,** building more affordable housing, and the rehabilitation of older buildings and structures with the goal of promoting **sustainability** at the local and neighborhood levels. Turning down free money is hard but, understanding what a mixed-use development is, could make it much easier.

Mixed-use development is part of Agenda 21's plan for **walkability**, taking people out of their cars, placing them in high-rise complexes where their jobs and businesses will be on the ground floors and their homes will be above. No more driving, no need for parking garages, mass transit use if available, or just plain moving only within walking or biking distance, while giving the land back to wilderness.

To put this absurd need of returning land to wilderness into proper perspective, consider that 77-84 percent of Americans live on 3 percent of United States' land mass. Sixteen percent of Americans live in rural areas. Ninety-five percent of America's land is rural.

Three million dollars of this HUD grant money will be awarded to jurisdictions with populations fewer than 50,000 via the Preferred Sustainability Status (PSS).

The HUD program is in its second year of existence, was built on the Partnership for **Sustainable** Communities, and was launched by President Obama in June 2009 between HUD, the Department of Transportation, and EPA "to provide more **sustainable** housing and transportation choices for families and lay the foundation for a 21st century economy."

What kind of economy is a "21st century economy?" I thought we had plenty of transportation choices in a free market capitalist society that "we the people" prefer. All Americans should think of COMMUNISM and LOSS OF FREEDOM when they hear and read the word **sustainable** in any sentence.

A website was launched to promote the forced "fundamental change" of our society by the scary Partnership, community by community, www.sustainablecommunities.gov. Last year 80 communities around the country have already used grant money for "sustainable communities' future."

Another website, www.fedcenter.gov, has ample information and governmental links to **sustainability** and Agenda 21.

On June 29, 2011, White House Council on Environmental Quality (CEQ) announced its second annual GreenGov Symposium which took place on October 31-November 2, 2011 in D.C. Leaders from government, private sector, non-profits, and academia discussed job creation, growing clean energy, and curb pollution. I know that governments never create jobs, just government bureaucracies. Will this new clean energy meet the needs of our huge economy? Since it is so much more expensive than fossil fuels energy, I seriously doubt it.

The GreenGov Symposium was sponsored by the White House Council on Environmental Quality (CEQ) and the Association of Climate Change Officers (ACCO). Nancy Sutley, chair of CEQ said, "GreenGov Symposium will help agencies deliver on President Obama's commitment to save money and reduce waste by increasing energy efficiency and reducing harmful pollution through **sustainable practices** in government operations." Agenda 21 marched on.

President Obama signed Executive Order 13514 in October 2009 to support the growth of 21st century clean energy economy. At the 2011 symposium, participants shared "**sustainability** challenges and best practices, and discussed cutting-edge approaches to achieving the Federal performance goals set by President Obama."

Hosted by George Mason University, the first GreenGov Symposium of October 2010 had "1,400 representatives from across all levels of government, the private sector and the non-profit community to shape the future of Federal Government **sustainability.**"

Program topics included **sustainability solutions** on clean energy, climate and adaptation, greening the supply chain, **sustainable buildings**, **sustainable communities**, water, zero waste, etc.

The White House Committee on Environmental Quality (CEQ) provided keynote speakers at last year's GreenGov Symposium held at George Mason University:

- Steven Chu, Secretary of U.S. Department of Energy that provides/produces no energy except pure research
- Tom Vilsack, Secretary of U.S. Department of Agriculture
- Janine Benyus, President of Biomimicry Institute

I was curious about the Association of Climate Change Officers (ACCO) since global warming has been debunked and they have now changed their name to climate change. This organization has steep joining fees and a very interesting Advisory Board with ties to U.N. Agenda 21 organizations and governing bodies:

- EPA staff
- AIG Sustainability Steering Committee (who knew that an insurance giant had a sustainability agenda?)
- U.N. Director of Partnership Development for Energy and Climate **Sustainable Development**
- Earth Institute at Columbia University Director
- Seattle Climate Partnership Director
- Chairman of the Science Advisory Council for the International SeaKeepers Society (a 501c3 non-profit)
- Illinois EPA chair
- California Air Resources Board Executive Officer
- American Carbon Registry Director
- Applied Materials, Inc. Senior Director **for Sustainability**
- VP of Trucost (built the world's most extensive database of over 700 emissions and pollutants of over 4,500 public companies around the world)
- USA VP of Carbon Disclosure Project
- **Sustainability** Action and Education Chair

- California's Secretary for EPA
- Carbon Disclosure New York
- Margery Moore, designer, developer, and implementer of environmental compliance, and **sustainability** for NGOs, governments, and corporations (NGOs are non-government organizations)

For those citizens who are non-believers or sitting on the fence, UN Agenda 21's implementation has accelerated in the last two years at unbelievable speed: No Child Left Inside Act of Maryland (forcing environmental literacy in order to graduate from high school), White House Rural Council, Codex Alimentarius, Smart Growth Plans in most municipalities and localities, social engineering, **sustainable** development at every level of government, **sustainable** rural communities, ICLEI (International Council for Local Environmental Initiatives) increased membership, Watershed Protection Plans, Habitat Conservation Plans, County Parks and Open Space Plans, all implemented without Congressional approval. Fifty percent of private land in the country is slated to be conserved or protected – that may be your land, your home, or your farm.

When are Americans going to wake up that state and local representatives with vested Marxist and/or capitalist interests are going to "fundamentally change America" and the way we live without our approval? Perhaps when they lose their lands, homes, electricity, and air conditioning? Local and state politicians should not be allowed to enforce ICLEI's agenda, it is a violation of our Constitution.

UN's Agenda 21 Forcing Society
Back to the Ghetto

I came across an article from Baton Rouge, LA, with a sugary title like an elementary singsong, "Grow Forth and Prosper." Then I zoomed in on the subtitle, "Smart Growth proponents say building up may save Baton Rouge – but only if we do it the right way." I am not sure which way the author understood it, but it was obviously the UN Agenda 21 way.

Such articles supporting Smart Growth, Smart Meters, and Sustainable Development have started to appear across the country with regularity in support of UN Agenda 21's goals of de-developing our capitalist economy, control and reduce population, control land use, and redistribution of wealth, under the guise of protecting our environment. Slowly but surely, they have made great strides across the U.S. with very little opposition or understanding from the population. The articles do not mention UN Agenda 21 at all, just benign euphemisms associated with environmentalist issues.

Smart Meters were installed around the country with power company bribes ranging from $40-100, an idea sold to customers as good for the environment and saving electricity. Now people are suffering six hours every day when their electricity is remotely cut off at consumption peaks. Customers were told and bullied that opting out is not an option. Who decided that a homeowner could not opt out of a particular device?

How many people will have to die of heat stroke? How will electronics fare, especially computers? What would happen to food and medicine in the fridge? How will the A/C units cope with power surges? How will computers fare in hot and humid rooms? How will homes deal with the humidity that will build up in basements since de-humidifiers will be idle? How will sump pumps route water away from home foundations? There will be a lot of mold growing.

UN Agenda 21 elites have decided that America has too much urban sprawl; we have to cut back, de-grow, and return to the pre-car era of the early 20th century. The Baton Rouge author enthusiastically opines that urban sprawl makes us "suffer economically and in terms of peace of mind." Who knew that giving up our cars, suburban homes, and moving into high-rise tenements suggested by architects of UN Agenda 21, will make us happier and pain free?

In the author's liberal view, suburbia has caused a bankrupt bus system, ghost neighborhoods, crumbling infrastructure within the city, "while development in the surrounding suburbs was flourishing." Could the high crime rate, high school dropout rate, drug dealing and use, lack of societal responsibility for one's children, lack of work ethic, the creation of perennial welfare generations be the reasons for the inner city blight and decay?

The Center for Planning and Excellence, a UN Agenda 21 approved organization, held its annual Smart Growth Summit, "a conference of some of the most brilliant and bold minds – both local and national – in urban land use and development in Baton Rouge." The local and national minds that were making policy for Baton Rouge were driven by UN Agenda 21 goals of Sustainability and Smart Growth.

Smart Growth is indeed the "anti-American" dream. The ideals of a white picket fence and a two-car garage have not lost their appeal to most Americans. People from around the world come to the U.S. to pursue the opportunity to have the American dream – freedom from oppression, the right to worship freely, education, and a home of their own. They did not escape poverty to be satisfied with the dreams chosen for them by the One World Government elites. They do not wish to be wards of the state from cradle to grave.

Cities are aligning with the tenets of Smart Growth, moving people from suburbs, from their homes, from their cars, into high-rise ghetto tenements within five-minute walk or bike from work, shops, school. Buses and trains will become the main mode of longer distance transportation because UN Agenda 21 says that agricultural land must be reclaimed for unspoiled nature and roads will be abandoned and no longer repaired. Nobody objects to walking, however, people will be trapped like rats in a five-minute walk maze - your daily world. No more spur of the moment road trips, no more hopping in your car for a 25-mile ride to a friend's house.

The Dulles Corridor in D.C., when completed, will charge such an expensive toll in one direction that locals will be forced out of their cars and into trains. The developers do not really care as long as their investment pays off.

Traditional washing machines are fast disappearing. New ones come with preset water levels and detergent type, in compliance with UN Agenda 21 goals and parameters.

The Baton Rouge author repeats the pre-scripted sales pitch of UN Agenda 21. Non-governmental organizations (NGOs) with "public-private partnerships are the key to establishing successful smart growth projects." She has no idea what it entails, it just sounds good, warm and fuzzy.

We live in a thriving country, with thriving communities and, until recently, a thriving economy that bureaucrats and politicians in Washington have destroyed with their spending and political pandering, we do not need to re-engineer the UN's ill-designed idea of "sustainable thriving community." There is no such thing – most developing countries that have concocted the UN Agenda 21 monstrosity live in substandard conditions because corrupt politicians have filled their bank accounts with wealth stolen from the UN coffers.

Now they want more from the United States because we are wealthy in their view and we created our wealth not through hard work, entrepreneurship, risk-taking, excellent work ethic, and productivity. In their opinion, we did it at the expense of poor people.

All these grants given to communities and local governments come with strings attached - the loss of freedom, land use, cars, and homes. Taking funds away from repairing and building roads in order to buy more buses and to build high-rise tenements is not the way most Americans want to live.

Deliberate tenement development is new to Louisiana and everywhere else, that is why they have to lie to people in order to build **consensus**. Building consensus is the tactic used by UN Agenda 21 to pass its illegal goals across communities in the U.S. under the pretense that it was the community's idea, they voted on it, and they passed it, when in reality, the opposite is true. The ideas and plans came from higher-ups in the UN Agenda 21. "The United Nations has got you fooled. No matter how smart you think you are, it's got you hoodwinked." (Michael Benson)

"The smart growth philosophy is rooted in urban designs that dominated the first half of the 20th century, before the automobile became a household commodity." Why would anyone want to go back to those times, destroying one hundred years of progress?

UN Agenda 21 Smart Growth has five important tenets:

1. **Existing Infrastructure** (rehabilitate areas already established in the city) Americans love their independence and living on their farms, why force them into ghettoes?

2. **Low Auto Dependence** (no driving within a community, offering trolleys, buses, walkways, bike paths, rails) What would happen if I don't want to give up my car, I cannot bike, walk, take bus, or train?

3. **High Density** (anti-sprawl, plucking us from the suburbs and placing us forcefully into tenements with specific boundaries)

4. **Mixed-Use, Mixed-Income** (multi-income community with multi-problems, disease born by overcrowding and close proximity, schools, supermarkets, retails, pharmacies, and work within the confines of the boundaries of the community; if it sounds Orwellian, it is)

5. **Whole Community** (all this crowding and proximity is supposed to create a warm and fuzzy sense of togetherness and community) Yes, I remember the sense of community we had in our communist tenements - noise, dirt, disease, spitting, everybody spying on everybody else for a little extra food handouts from the ruling elite, beatings, and disappearances.

After the secret deliberations of the Constitutional Convention of 1787, a Mrs. Powell of Philadelphia asked Benjamin Franklin, "Well, Doctor, what have we got, a republic or a monarchy?" Franklin responded with no hesitation, "A republic, if you can keep it."

It appears that we are not going to keep our republic, we are headed into uncharted territory. The sad and frustrating thing is that Americans are acquiescing either because they are uninformed, have not studied history, are not paying attention, or are refusing to believe the evidence before their eyes.

The New American Dream as Envisioned by UN Agenda 21

When liberals are not destroying private property or setting fire to private businesses to protest the very capitalism that afforded them the freedom, time, and money to be idle and live off the hard work of others, they come up with ideas to "fundamentally change" and redefine the American dream. After all, they are the ultimate experts at everything - what we should eat, how and where we should live, how we learn, what we read, what we drive, what we watch, where we pray, if we are allowed to pray, what kind of medicines we can take, and what doctors we can see.

They think other primitive cultures are superior to our culture. They have been taught America is evil. America and its people have to change into the vision that only liberals can conjure up in conjunction with various nefarious United Nations third world organizations and countries.

The history and reality changers invent, write, and produce cartoon videos like the "Story of Stuff Project," widely distributed and viewed in classrooms across the country with the goal to bamboozle children into believing that capitalism is evil and our way of life is destroying the planet at this very moment if we do not do something about it. Children are impressionable, trusting, naïve, gullible, and listen to misguided authority; they do not know how to verify false statements.

The "Story of Stuff" 20 minute-video plants the idea of socialism and communism as being the only way to live and save our planet from our laser-guided, capitalist destruction. We consume too much, they say. We have to return to a simpler life, to the pre-car, pre-technology era, to a time of equality that only exists in their deluded minds. In progressive views communism is wonderful; it only failed repeatedly throughout history because the right person was not in charge. This is the definition of insanity; repeat the same mistake, hoping to obtain a different result.

The Center for a New American Dream is promoting the redefinition of the American Dream. They must have had a revelation one day that they were worthless pawns in the huge universe that needed rearranging on the chess board of life.

"One of the root causes of our environmental problems is hyper-consumption. We simply buy too much of what we don't really need." We need a simpler living, the center's definition of simpler living. Pursuing this simpler living may be sailing around the world in an expensive sailboat to find yourself. How many Americans could actually afford a sailboat much less consider such a lifestyle change without a considerable trust fund? It is simply incredible and egotistical in its lack of work ethic of adventure-seekers and "simple living" dreamers who fund their adventures with other people's hard work and money.

There you have it, Nancy Pelosi's advice in action, you can take time to find yourself and dream while the nanny state or a trust fund provides your sustenance and support.

The environmental and progressive Center for a New American Dream founded in 1997 promotes "a more socially and ecologically balanced society." "We seek to change social norms around consumption and consumerism" and replace it with community action and collaborative communities. Collaborative communities, right out of UN Agenda 21, create local initiatives, ecological sustainability, livability, and engage local governments to embrace sustainability. "We seek to cultivate a new American dream—one that emphasizes community, ecological sustainability, and a celebration of non-material values." It sounds so selfless and gratifying. What non-profits and grants are financing their non-material lifestyle, salaries, and agenda? The staff is composed of community organizers, activists, and environmentalists.

The list of those who endorse the center reads like a who is who among Hollywood progressives including Robert Reich, former U.S. Secretary of Labor. Robert Reich says, "The Center is forging the way toward a more **equitable and sustainable** future." Meryl Streep suggests that we should change our consumer behavior in order to restore balance to the planet. I promise to do it right after she changes her lavish Hollywood lifestyle.

A Democrat politician urges consumers to protect the environment and promote social justice. United Nations Agenda 21 believes that wealth and consumption were built on the backs of the poor and must thus be re-distributed from the rich to those who decided to work less, study less, and play the game of **victimology.**

Ed Begley Jr. talks about the "orgy of consumerism" but I have not heard or seen him donate his wealth made in Hollywood. It was poor and ordinary Americans who paid to watch his movies – capitalism in action. When he does give away his last penny, the rest of us, evil capitalists will do the same.

The Center for a New American Dream is an organization that promotes at the local and national level the UN's Agenda 21. It is headquartered in Charlottesville, Virginia and offers summer internships to our naïve youth who will become tomorrow's UN Agenda 21 slaves.

DICED Is UN's Environmental Constitution for the World

I am sure there are many Americans who have no idea nor care what "The Draft International Covenant on Environment and Development" (DICED) is. They should. The Draft Covenant is the "Environmental Constitution of Global Governance."

The first version of the Covenant was presented to the United Nations in 1995 on the occasion of its fiftieth anniversary. It was hoped that it would become a negotiating document for a global treaty on environmental conservation and sustainable development.

The fourth version of the Covenant, issued on September 22, 2010, was written to control all development tied to the environment, "the highest form of law for all human activity.'

The Covenant's 79 articles, described in great detail in 242 pages, take Sustainable Development principles described in UN Agenda 21 and transform them into global law, which supersedes all constitutions including the U.S. Constitution.

All signatory nations, including the U.S., would become centrally planned, socialist countries in which all decisions would be made within the framework of Sustainable Development.

In collaboration with Earth Charter and Elizabeth Haub Foundation for Environmental Policy and Law from Canada, the Covenant was issued by the International Council on Environmental

Law (ICEL) in Bonn, Germany, and the International Union for Conservation of Nature (IUCN) with offices in Gland, Switzerland and Cambridge, UK.

Federal agencies that are members of the International Union for Conservation of Nature (IUCN) include U.S. Department of State, Commerce, Agriculture (Forest Service), Interior (Fish and Wildlife, National Park Service), and the Environmental Protection Agency (EPA). The same agencies are members of the White House Rural Council and the newly established White House Council on Strong Cities, Strong Communities (Executive Order, March 15, 2012).

The Draft Covenant is a blueprint "to create an agreed single set of fundamental principles like a 'code of conduct' used in many civil law, socialist, and theocratic traditions, which may guide States, intergovernmental organizations, and individuals."

The writers describe the Covenant as a "living document," a blueprint that will be adopted by all members of the United Nations. They say that global partnership is necessary in order to achieve Sustainable Development, by focusing on "social and economic pillars." The writers are very careful to avoid the phrase, "one world government." Proper governance is necessary on all levels, "from the local to the global." (p.36)

The Covenant underwent four writings, in 1995, 2000, 2004, and 2010, influenced by the Johannesburg World Summit on Sustainable Development, by ideas of development control and social engineering by the United Nations, "leveling the playing field for international trade, and having a common basis of future lawmaking."

Article 2 describes in detail "respect for all life forms."

Article 3 proposes that the entire globe should be under "the protection of international law."

Article 5 refers to "equity and justice," code words for socialism/communism.

Article 16 requires that all member nations must adopt environmental conservation into all national decisions.

Article 19 deals with "Stratospheric Ozone." **Rex communis** is the customary international law regime applicable to areas beyond national jurisdiction: in particular to the high seas and outer space." (p. 72)

Article 20 requires that all nations must "mitigate the adverse effects of climate change." If we ratify this document, we must thus fight a non-existent man-made climate change. (Alex Jones)

Article 31, "Action to Eradicate Poverty," requires the eradication of poverty by spreading the wealth from developed nations to developing countries.

Article 32 requires recycling, "consumption and production patterns."

Article 33, "Demographic policies," demands that countries calculate "the size of the human population their environment is capable of supporting and to implement measures that prevent the population from exceeding that level." In Malthusian model, humans were supposed to run out of food and starve to death. In a similar prediction, this document claims that the out-of control multiplication of humans can endanger the environment.

Article 34 demands the maintenance of an open and non-discriminatory international trading system in which "prices of commodities and raw materials reflect the full direct and indirect social and environmental costs of their extraction, production, transport, marketing, and where appropriate, ultimate disposal.. "The capitalist model of supply and demand pricing does not matter.

Article 37 discusses "Trans-boundary Environmental Effects and article 39 directs how "Trans-boundary Natural Resources" will be conserved, "quantitatively and qualitatively." According to the document, "conserve means managing human-induced processes and activities which may be damaging to natural systems in such a way that the essential functions of these systems are maintained."

Article 41 requires integrated planning systems, irrespective of administrative boundaries within a country, and is based on Paragraph 10.5 of Agenda 21, which seeks to "facilitate allocation of land to the uses that provide the greatest sustainable benefits and to promote the transition to a sustainable and integrated management of land resources." The impact assessment procedure is developed by the World Bank.

"Aquifers, drainage basins, coastal, marine areas, and any areas called ecological units must be taken into account when allocating land for municipal, agricultural, grazing, forestry, and other uses." Agricultural subsidies are discouraged, as well as subsidizing private enterprises.

"Physical planning must follow an integrated approach to land use – infrastructure, highways, railways, waterways, dams, and harbors. Town and country planning must include land use plans elaborated at all levels of government."

"Sharing Benefits of Biotechnology" is a similar requirement to the Law of the Sea Treaty which demands that final products of research and development be used freely, no matter who develops an idea or how much it costs to bring that idea to the market.

Article 51 reveals that we will have to pay for these repressive new requirements while Article 52 shows that we must pay 0.7 percent of GDP for Official Development Assistance. This reaffirms the political commitment made in Paragraph 33.13 of UN Agenda 21 in 1992.

Article 69 deals with settlement of disputes by the Permanent Court of Arbitration, the International Court of Justice, and/or the International Tribunal for the Law of the Sea. This will supersede any court in the United States.

Article 71 describes the amendment process, which is submitted to the Secretary-General of the United Nations. UN Secretary-General would review the implementation of this document every five years.

Writers of the Draft Covenant include 19 U.S. professors of Law, Biology, Natural Resources, Urban Planning, Theology, Environmental Ethics, two General Counsel Representatives from the Environmental Protection Agency, the chair of the IUCN Ethics Working Group, two attorneys in private practice in the U.S., a judge from the International Court of Justice, a U.S. High Seas Policy advisor of the IUCN Global Marine Programme, foreign dignitaries, ambassadors, and 13 members of the UN Secretariat, including the Chairman, Dr. Wolfgang E. Burhenne. (2006-present)

Because this Draft Covenant has a Preamble and 79 articles, it is obviously intended to be a "world constitution for global governance," an onerous way to control population growth, re-distribute wealth, force social and "economic equity and justice," economic control, consumption control, land and water use control, and re-settlement control as a form of social engineering.

Global Reporting Initiative, Sustainability, And The New Space Race

America was founded on the principle that private property is sacred. Americans cannot conceive their country without the right to own property. As they go about their daily lives, the United Nations Agenda 21 is methodically chipping away at our country's solid foundation.

Under the guise of protecting the environment, social justice, water conservation, resources, reducing carbon footprint, reducing the use of electricity, smart grid, smart meters, cutting down the use of fossil fuels, separating people from their cars in favor of mass transit, biking and walking within five minutes of residence, returning land to wilderness by moving large rural and urban populations into high rise tenements in green zones, the UN is taking over our lives.

UN Agenda 21 marches on in spite of the many revelations that global warming, climate change scare tactics, faulty data, and faux academic research from the University of East Anglia have been debunked.

U.S. Energy Secretary Chu, promoting engineering education in Portland, spoke about Sustainability as the next great space race. Not only was he promoting engineering when our space program no longer exists, but his remarks on green energy came on the heels of three bankruptcies of "clean energy" companies that are yet to deliver any clean energy or provide the millions of jobs needed to replace the current ones lost during President Obama's misadministration of our fossil fuel-based economy. The most famous company that failed in spite of heavy stimulus dollars was Solyndra.

Ethanol-producers of "clean energy" were complaining that the price of corn has gone up and supply of corn has diminished, hurting their ability to produce ethanol. At the same time, our food supply of corn has diminishedl, and some countries are experiencing shortages of their staple food and higher prices. This is one indication that we are definitely nowhere near replacing fossil fuels as a large scale, cheap source of energy without bankrupting our entire economy.

UN Agenda 21's sustainability everything is not about safeguarding the environment and clean energy, it is about economic power and control. It is about brokering and laundering carbon credit scams, about world dominance and destruction of the largest economy on the planet. The U.S. is the only country standing in the way of a one world global government under the aegis of the United Nations.

Every day a new facet of UN Agenda 21 comes into focus. They call us "stakeholders," although few of us have any idea what is going on. Take for instance, the Global Reporting Initiative. Located in Amsterdam, GRI encourages organizations to report (snitch) on Sustainable Development compliance in their countries. The portal supporters of this 'voluntary' Sustainable Development reporting network are TATA, Microsoft, and HP.

The list of supporters include, among many European nations, World Bank, Charles Stewart Mott Foundation, John D. and Catherine T. MacArthur Foundation, Ford Foundation, Bill and Melinda Gates Foundation, Rockefeller Brothers Fund, Spencer T. and Ann W. Olin Foundation, EPA, and the Soros Foundation.

GRI organizes every two years the Amsterdam Global Conference on Sustainability and Transparency, a love fest of sustainability reporting. GRI has divided the globe into five sectors overseen by stakeholders and council members: Africa, Asia Pacific/Oceania, Latin America/Caribbean, North America/Europe, and West Asia. GRI has "synergies" with the Earth Charter Initiative, International Finance Corporation (a World Bank group), the International

Organization for Standardization, and UN Conference on Trade and Development.

"The mission of the Earth Charter Initiative is to promote the transition to sustainable ways of living and a global society founded on a shared ethical framework that includes respect and care for the community of life, ecological integrity, universal human rights, respect for diversity, economic justice, democracy, and a culture of peace."

We live in a constitutional republic not a democracy. We do not wish to live in a global society and we are not global citizens. We live in the United States of America and we safeguard its freedoms. Human rights are respected in America, unlike the tin pot dictatorships that are members of human rights committees at the United Nations yet are the worst offenders and violators of basic human rights, especially for women. We are so diverse to the point that political correctness is stifling free speech and destroying our society. We do not want Fabian socialist "economic justice" that involves the taking of wealth from producers and giving it to non-producers who are satisfied with waiting on handouts from the government. It is hard to imagine an American who does not want to live in peace; unfortunately, we are at war with a hostile theocratic ideology and society and thus, as the Romans very wisely said, "Si vis pacem, para bellum," if you want peace, prepare for war. Should United Nations dictate to the rest of the world what economic justice is? We do not wish to receive lectures on respect for diversity from UN totalitarian governments that disrespect women, forbid other religions, stone people to death for minor infractions, genitally mutilate women, kill homosexuals, and repress minorities through genocide.

GRI wants to integrate sustainability into business strategy and management. I had no idea that investment is "increasingly guided by environmental, social, and governance factors." I thought investment was guided by the selfish capitalist desire to make money and, in the process, provide a good product or service that people need, want, and are willing to purchase.

Public reporting on "social responsibility performance" by employees, local communities, investors, and regulators is highly recommended. We had informants under the communist system – it allowed the totalitarian government to better control the masses. In capitalism we have whistleblower laws; we do not need UN's rules to control us through organized snitching. The real ultimate goal of GRI is to spread the wealth and arrest development in countries like the United States.

Do we really need the United Nations to regulate our country, corporations, and citizens in every way into poverty because third world nations think that we are not good stewards of the environment and must thus be controlled and snitched on if we don't comply? Do we need United Nations Environment Programme (UNEP), based in Nairobi, Kenya, to be our "environmental conscience?"

GRI partnered with the UN Global Compact and derived its ten goals from the Rio Declaration on Environment and Development of 1992 (UN Agenda 21).

Therein resides the rub; although they use the word **voluntary** through a very cleverly forced "consensus," many of the UN Agenda 21 goals have been adopted at local levels without any input from the population. Interested parties who stood to gain financially and politicians chose smart growth, smart meters, smart grid, land grabs, land stewardship and preservation, and water conservation in the name of the taxpayers. Their choices and decisions are now being pushed in every county and state that has adopted UN Agenda 21 initiatives through generous government grants and ICLEI partners.

As I searched many websites to compile my reports, the encroachment of United Nation's Agenda 21 is painfully evident. Sustainability Departments have been formed at universities across the world, offering degrees in sustainable everything, including engineering degrees in Aeolian (wind) and solar energy. Everyone knows that we cannot replace the current need of energy in our economy alone with wind and solar energy generation, it is insufficient. Look up the words sustainable development, sustainability, smart growth, environmental stewardship, green agenda, and just one site, www.fedcenter.gov, and you will see how many organizations already have plans in place to control everything that we do under the UN umbrella of a one world government.

Oceans and Regionalism

The World Oceans Summit in Singapore was the platform for United Nations World Bank to announce its latest assault on sovereign economic decisions and freedom. The oceans are suddenly very sick and "we need coordinated global action to restore our oceans to health," said World Bank president Robert Zoellick.

UN has decided that we need a new partnership to "confront the problems of over-fishing, marine degradation, and loss of habitat." To achieve this goal, Zoellick proposed $300 million in "catalytic finance" from a coalition of countries, scientific centers, NGOs, international organizations, foundations, and the private sector.

Knowledge, experience, expertise, and investment will be gathered around a set of agreed upon goals. His next sentence, revealed the creator of this new scheme, the United Nations with its Agenda 21. Another $1.2 billion had to be raised, he said, "to support healthy and sustainable oceans." A "sustainable" anything is the buzzword for Agenda 21. The final total would be $1.5 billion in new commitments over five years. The group reconvened in April 2012 in Washington, D.C. for further lobbying of U.S. funds.

Zoellick suggested that marine protected areas should be 5 percent not just 2 percent. After all, 12 percent of land is protected. The earth's water mass is so much larger, they must control more."The world's oceans are in danger, "send out the S-O-S, we need to save our seas."

One billion people in developing countries depend on fish and seafood for their primary source of protein and half a billion depend on fishing for their livelihood. Fishing represents 80 percent of export for Pacific Island states and coastal nations. It is abundantly clear that this new platform is another UN Agenda 21 initiative to spread the wealth from developed countries to developing nations.

If we consider the Law of the Sea Treaty (LOST) which aims to control mineral and oil exploration in oceans, and oceanic passage under the United Nations control with its "Agency," the Biosphere land preserves and corridors, population density controls, rezoning of living areas, restricted mobility through decreased usage of fossil fuels as a means of locomotion, and now control of fishing on the oceans and passage through territorial waters, it is evident that United Nations wants to control every aspect of our lives.

Additionally, across the U.S. efforts are underway to pass Regional plans that erase boundaries between cities, counties, and states. "We are losing our ability to influence our government policies at the same time that we are being solicited for our opinion." Rosa Koire explains in her book, Behind the Green Mask: U.N. Agenda 21, that this is the Delphi method of manipulating and controlling groups that may protest.

HB 430 will expand the "Regional Cooperation Incentive Fund" and allow the fund to offer an increased amount of government grant money to planning commissions that "consolidate or coordinate" with other local planners, thus regionalize.

Regionalization is a step towards globalization. It is an unelected, unaccountable layer of government in which municipalities become borderless groups. The unelected individuals develop comprehensive plans of land use that supersede local laws and often disregard private property rights. This parasitic layer of government requires the local community to bring their laws and zoning in line with their dictates.

By 2050 there will be 11 Mega-Regions in the United States, including parts of Canada and Mexico (www.America2050.org). The regional planning sign-up and ensnaring of cities is found at ICLEI's website (www.iclei.org) and the United Nations' website.(www.un.org/esa/dsd/agenda21/)
The adoption date of Regional plans all over the United States is 2013. (www.un.org/esa/dsd/agenda21/)

The Regional plans are implemented in order to reduce greenhouse gas emissions, to expand public transportation, and to fund low-income housing, with slight variations, depending on the area. High-density areas, restrictions on building because of urban sprawl, Smart Growth development, reduced or no car usage, bike paths are some of the issues presented. Light rail and high speed trains are the common denominator of the Mega-Regions.

According to the Post Sustainability Institute and its Executive Director, Rosa Koire, all Mega-Region "Plans give power to regional transportation and planning boards through federal and state fund disbursement. Housing and transportation are linked and population projections are hugely inflated."

Examples of plans around the country that include the word "vision," a buzzword of UN Agenda 21, are:
- One Valley One Vision (Santa Clarita Valley, Ca; Montana; Las Cruces, New Mexico)
- Nine Counties One Vision (Tennessee)
- One Region One Vision (New York, Indiana)
- Our Florida Our Vision
- One Bay Area (9 counties and San Francisco Bay area)
- Six Towns One Vision (Lycoming County)
- Five Counties One Vision (Minnesota)
- Four States One Vision (Oklahoma, Arkansas, Missouri, Kansas)

Citizens who accept these plans and do not fight back, are accepting a foreign entity's idea of what should happen to state and local governments – the installation of an unelected regional regime of the UN Agenda 21/Sustainable Development/ICLEI (International Council on Local Environmental Initiatives) and the destruction of traditional, American elected state and local governments.

Environmentalists are still pushing the global warming agenda although it had been revealed as highly inaccurate. Thirty thousand temperature readings all over the world have actually shown a global cooling since 1997. There is just too much money to be made from cap and trade and carbon taxes charged to hapless citizens all over the world to give up on the crafty idea of global warming.

The climate scientist Richard Lindzen of MIT declared that global warming is not backed by "settled science." "Claims that the earth has been warming, that there is a Greenhouse Effect, and that man's activity have contributed to warming are trivially true but essentially meaningless." The CO2 doubling in the last 150 years represents a change in temperature rise of seven or eight tenths of one degree Celsius. Dr. Richard Lindzen further explained that CO2 represented a two percent change in radiation. When the sun was 20-30 percent cooler, about two billion years ago, the planet's temperature was the same. Dr. Lindzen continued that the slide Al Gore presented, showing melting ice caps, disappearing icebergs, receding glaciers, and rising sea levels was published by the U.S. Weather Bureau in 1922.

According to Rodney Atkinson, if Dr. Lindzen is right, we will never be able to calculate the trillions that have been spent on the advice of 'scientists in the service of politics.'

Americans are either overwhelmed, believe the media, or are blissfully unaware of the UN Agenda 21's highly successful attacks on our country. The question remains, are we going to be effective in fighting back the Green Environmental Monster, this multi-faceted assault on our freedom and our way of life? Are we going to roll back and wait to be completely taken over?

Food, Codex Alimentarius, and Initium

We are a nation in great decline, attacked from many fronts by issues born at least fifty years ago and bearing fruit now, and by individuals who do not hold our nation's interests at heart, the so called internationalists/globalists. They are simply environmental pirates, plundering our economy in the name of caring for the earth.

We are plagued by corruption at all levels of government, the shredding of our Constitution, by stoked hatred, class envy, drugs, anarchists, sexual deviance, communist Wall Street Occupiers, violence, anti-Americanism, perverse Hollywood lifestyles, indolence, anti-Christianity, Sharia Law, UN Agenda 21, and communism worship.

The incremental loss of our private property, land, freedoms, and sovereignty are the most glaring symbols of our decline. Many factors will combine to lead to our eventual demise as a superpower.

History repeats itself and we are not paying attention. We have stopped teaching long ago any meaningful and truthful history to our children. We have allowed public schools to replace our Judeo-Christian teaching with Marxist ideology and worship.

Ten million new acres of land have been "voluntarily conserved" and "saved from development" since 2005, according to a five-year census recently released by the Land Trust Alliance, one of the 1,700 private land trusts. By 2010, economic development and freedom of movement was no longer allowed on 47 million acres of land.

The world was stunned when the "Eternal City," Rome, which had stood unconquered for 800 years, fell under the occupation of the barbarian Alaric the Goth. St. Jerome, born and raised in Rome, wrote from Bethlehem, "When the brightest light on the whole Earth was extinguished, when the Roman Empire was deprived of its head, when, to speak more correctly, the whole world perished in one city, I was dumb with silence."

The Western Roman Empire lingered on for 66 more years until 476 A.D. when Romulus Augustus, the last emperor, was deposed by his Germanic commanders.

The Eastern Empire survived until 1453 when it was captured by Ottoman Empire. It called itself the Roman Empire but it was Greek in life and language.

Alaric wanted to share the Roman way of life, had been asking for years for the title of allied commander, and wanted land for his men. Despair and deception drove him to attack Rome.

Interestingly, even before attacking and conquering Rome, the Goths had been slowly adopting Roman customs, while many generations of Romans living in distant parts of the empire were influenced more and more by barbarians. Ever more Roman soldiers were recruited from Germanic people who had no loyalty to Rome. You could say that the Romans were destroying themselves from within psychologically and demographically.

There are perhaps similarities between the fall of the Roman Empire and other empires whose influence waned in shorter time. Historians claim that empires tend to last on the average 250 years before decline, loss of power, or complete disappearance.

One of the threats that Romans faced was self-induced. Water was carried through lead pipes; Romans drank from lead cups, cooked in lead pipes, sweetened wine with lead oxide, and even used it as face and hair powder.

Archeological and written texts show that many Romans suffered from paralyzed limbs, headaches, listless, lack of energy, sterility, all classic symptoms of chronic lead poisoning. Excavations at Circencester in southern England, found in the period 1969-1976, 450 skeletons in a Roman cemetery dating from the late fourth and early fifth centuries. The bones of adults contained ten times the amount of lead and children had even more.

Evidence suggests that several emperors encouraged Romans to have children, declining population perhaps resulting from drinking lead poison to death and extinction. Fortunately, the Eastern Roman Empire had fewer lead mines and used earthenware for pottery.

In a way, we are as unaware of potential toxins in our food supply and blissfully ignorant as the Romans were about their use of lead. Our global food production and safety is being watched and augmented via Codex Alimentarius (Latin for "Book of Food"), proposed by the Food and Agriculture Organization (FAO) and World Health Organization in 1963 under the United Nations umbrella.

The Codex Alimentarius' approved substance, initium, was first introduced in Romania on December 31, 2009 when the Boc government was asked by the European Union to begin using it on grapes, potatoes, tomatoes, cucumbers, and onions under the name Enervin and Zampro. Instead of lead, the offending substance was initium.

I am not suggesting that initium is lead, but it has the potential to alter our food supply in a fundamental way, possibly damaging our cells, along with genetically engineered plants and seeds, and coupled with the control of vitamins and nutritional supplements.

Initium is a new class of chemicals imposed by Codex Alimentarius as a fungicide; additionally, it accelerates the growth rate of crops. "Initium is an innovative fungicidal active ingredient developed by BASF." First registrations have been achieved in Romania, the Netherlands, and the UK. Other countries are slated to follow, Germany, France, USA, and Canada. (BASF website)

The idea behind using chemical substances such as initium under Codex Alimentarius is that the earth cannot feed the entire globe naturally, and we must resort to artificial means through chemicals and genetic engineering in order to obtain higher crop yields, especially since we are competing with animals for scarce resources.

Governments deride as conspiracy theorists those who say that the use of initium and genetic engineering would reduce the globe's population through increased rates of cancer. Independent unofficial research claims that initium causes higher rates of colon cancer by as much as 65 percent more. One milligram of initium requires an entire year to be eliminated from the body. I have not found a second reliable source to corroborate this claim. If produce is eaten daily, initium will never be eliminated, accelerating cell growth into tumors, similarly to the accelerated growth in vegetable cells. Romanian authorities and farmers are happy that initium will double crop yields in a short period.

Codex Alimentarius began when the United Nations authorized the World Health Organization and the Food and Agriculture Organization to develop a universal food code in order to "harmonize" regulations for dietary supplements worldwide and set international safety standards for the purpose of international trade. When Big Pharma stepped in, Codex began focusing not so much on food safety but on controlling vitamins and food supplements.

Codex Alimentarius supersedes U.S. domestic laws without the American people's voice or vote. Under the terms of the Uruguay round of GATT (General Agreement on Tariffs and Trade), which created the World Trade Organization (WTO), the United States agreed to harmonize its domestic laws to the international standards. Standards for dietary supplements developed by the United Nation's Codex Alimentarius Commission's Committee on Nutrition and Foods for Special Dietary Use are included.

Our federal government must change federal laws and require state and local governments to change their laws in accordance with international law. "Members are fully responsible under this Agreement for the observance of all provisions… members shall formulate and implement positive measures and mechanisms in support of the observance of the provisions…by other than central government bodies." (WTO TBT Agreement at Article 3.5)

If we allow United Nations, the World Trade Organization, and the World Health Organization to control our food, they control our people, our freedom, and our population. Consequences of such control:

- Genetically engineered or altered foods, supplements, seeds and pesticides will be sold worldwide with or without labeling.
- Dietary supplements would not be sold for preventive or therapeutic use.
- Low doses will be sold by Big Pharma at higher potencies and higher prices.
- Prescriptions will be required for higher potencies.
- Garlic and peppermint could be classified as drugs or a third category (neither food nor drug) that only Big Pharma could regulate or sell.

-   New dietary supplements would be banned unless approved by Codex Alimentarius

Vitamin C above 200 mg, vitamin E above 45 IUs, vitamin B1 over 2.4 mg, and other vitamins in normal doses are illegal in Norway and Germany. The Norway pharmaceutical company, Shering-Plough, controls the production of Echinacea tincture, ginkgo, and other herbs.

Paul Hellyer stated in his book, *The Evil Empire*, "Codex Alimentarius is supported by international banks and multinational corporations… and is in reality a bill of rights for these banks and the corporations they control. It will hand over our sovereign rights concerning who may or may not invest in our countries to an unelected world organization run by big business."

It is time to wake up, take control back from the United Nations before we become another "has been" superpower or worse yet, a modern extinguished Roman Empire.

Global Warming Psychological Babble

The global warming alarmists have become so desperate in light of ever-increasing numbers of skeptics that they are trying to tie everything to global warming. The Securities and Exchange Commission published a document, describing how publicly traded companies should apply existing disclosure rules to the risk that climate change developments may have on their businesses. ("Commission Guidance Regarding Disclosure Related to Climate Change," January 27, 2010)

In response to this resource-wasteful guidance, Senator John Barrasso and Representative Bill Posey of the 112th Congress introduced similar bills, S. 1393 and H.R. 2603, prohibiting the enforcement of the SEC's climate change disclosure guidance. Companies have no experience in the so-called risks associated with climate change, there is no tangible actual or potential reputational harm from climate change, and the whole process is highly speculative to say the least.

The most egregious stretch of manufactured global warming effects is a 55-page report published in February 2012 by the National Wildlife Federation titled, "The Psychological Effects of Global Warming on the United States: And Why the U.S. Mental Health Care System is Not Adequately Prepared."

Prepared by a forensic psychiatrist and an attorney who adapted in 2006 Al Gore's book and film, "An Inconvenient Truth," into a training course curriculum, the lengthy psychobabble, a "national forum and research report," chastises Americans for "the adolescent-like disregard for the dangers we are warned of, driving greenhouse gases up with only casual concern."

We are asked "To find a place in our hearts that mobilizes us to fly into action, forewarned, determined, and relentless." We are probed with very childish questions, "what would the rest of the world think of us," "where will we be safe," "how will we feel about ourselves?"

Rational adults do not care what the rest of the world thinks. Americans feel safe unless environmentalists who treat us like children want to alter our lives fundamentally in the image of their worldview. We feel quite good about ourselves, although lately our egos have taken a beating, given the state of economic despair and purposeful destruction around us wrought by Congress who acts against "we the people" and by this Marxist administration.

The report is calling on "mental health professionals to focus on this, the social justice issue of all times." The twenty-four college professors, lawyers, doctors, and lobbyists who took part in the forum when this document was distributed represented medical colleges of psychiatry, the CDC, environmental NGOs, climate change lobbyists, and proponents of UN Agenda 21 Convention on Biodiversity.

The doomsday scenarios described in this document include many frightening and preposterous statements that have no backing in fact or science. Presented with a veneer of truth, supposed global warming effects on the psyche of the United States are presented as consensus opinion of people affiliated with environmental groups and universities. Consensus statements by public figures with an agenda are not facts.

The National Forum and Research Report is divided into an executive summary, six chapters, and a conclusion. (February 2012) The Executive Summary concentrates on "Climate change lessons from the severe weather of summer 2011." Violent weather is blamed on global warming instead of focusing on the fact that violent weather existed long before man's industrial revolution. They are confusing weather with climate.

The entire report ignores the fact that we have a much larger population today, almost 7 billion people in the path of harm in case of violent weather, we are more aware of occurring disasters, and we are almost instantly informed with a click of a button, as the news of any climactic event travels fast via Internet.

"Global warming...in the coming years... will foster public trauma, depression, violence, alienation, suicide, psychotic episodes, post-traumatic stress disorders and many other mental health-related conditions." (p. i) "The U.S. mental health care system is only minimally prepared to address the effects of global climate change-related disasters and incidents." (p. ii)

The writers are stretching the exploratory relationships between supposed global warming trends in climate and the state of the American public mental health. "An estimated 200 million Americans will be exposed to serious psychological distress from climate related events and incidents." (p. v) "Some 50 million elderly people, and America's 35 million low-income people will suffer a disproportionate amount of physical and psychological stress." (p. vi) By what scientific method have they ascertained these findings?

On pages v and xi, suggesting that "anxieties could increase with continuous and frequent media reports on the subject," (translation - ad nauseam reporting of one event on every alphabet soup channel for days on end), the Executive Summary recommends that "mental health practitioners, first responders and primary care professionals should have comprehensive plans and guidelines for climate change."

People have problems finding doctors to treat them for actual ailments, have no insurance, cannot afford insurance anymore because of the expensive and choice-robbing of Obamacare, and now professionals in the mental health community are urged to "shape the best language" to allow environmentalists to control people based on non-existent climate change illnesses? "Ramping up and sustaining pressure on public officials is imperative." (p. xiii)

Chapter 1 laments the fact that public policy leaders are not implementing legislative proposals to" reduce gas emissions enough to restore balance to our world and avoid long term environmental damage." (p. 3) Climate stability is so precarious, they say, that human stability and physical changes are "unprecedented in all of history." (p. 2)

Chapter 2 uses hurricane Katrina, one of thousands of hurricanes in our collective history, as an example of the manufactured word "solastalgia"…a "palpable sense of dislocation and loss that people feel when they perceive changes in their local environment as harmful." (p. 7) I must be feeling "solastalgic" every day then as environmentalists are pushing UN Agenda 21 undesirable and property-robbing changes on our society without our approval. The authors of the report, citing that 39 percent of Katrina evacuees experienced moderate PTSD, stated that "people suffer more from disasters that are "manmade" than they do from natural disasters. How do they know?

I have PTSD every time I see communism around me (manmade disaster) and I have experienced PTSD after a devastating earthquake and numerous hurricanes (natural disasters). I cannot honestly discern which one is affecting or has affected me more. To answer such a question would be my opinion, my perception, which is neither scientific nor a fact.

"Climate change is already having an impact on biodiversity,…loss of Arctic sea ice threatens biodiversity across an entire biome and beyond." (Secretariat of the Convention on Biological Diversity, Outlook 3, May 2010) I imagine that such bombastic statements have a frightening effect on ignorant and vulnerable adults and children who look up to authority for answers.

Chapter 3 discusses "traumatic global warming events" on vulnerable populations such as mentally ill, or the existence of epidemic levels of asthma among pre-school children. (p. 17)

Chapter 4 stretches global warming to unbelievable limits by connecting it to the stresses of war. "As the U.S. military looks ahead to the likely causes of war in the next 30 years…global warming is front and center." (p. 20) Citing Army statistics that 20 out of 100,000 soldiers have killed themselves, the report attributes war, strife, social injustice, and suicide rates to global warming caused by the rich. Redistribution of wealth will be necessary in order to avert the unleashing of global warming and the destruction of 30 percent of species and of humanity itself.

"The most profound danger to world peace in the coming years will stem not from the irrational acts of states or individuals but from the legitimate demands of the world's dispossessed. Of these poor and disenfranchised, the majority live a marginal existence in equatorial climates. Global warming, not of their making but originating with the wealthy few, will affect their fragile ecologies most. Their situation will be desperate and manifestly unjust." (p. 22)

Chapter 5 predicts nationwide anxiety. Dr. Eric Chivian postulates that the destructive potential of global warming is, in many ways, "greater than what we faced with nuclear war."(p. 27)

The authors suggest that a green economy could fix everything for the *common good*, "would provide opportunities for struggling American workers and some stalled or outmoded enterprises dependent on older industries and burning fossil fuels." (p. 28) Hapless Americans should not worry though, "the discipline of psychology can be used to uncover what the barriers are to reducing our carbon footprint and adopting a green lifestyle." (p. 31).

The nanny control state will take care of everyone and everything. All we have to do is relinquish our freedoms and cash completely. On my recent flight to Amsterdam, KLM was asking passengers to eliminate the carbon footprint that each passenger was incurring with that flight by making an in-flight donation, credit cards accepted. Where did the money go if anybody donated? The globalist environmental pirates gladly pocketed the cash.

Chapter 6 addresses the high cost of ignoring mental health and climate change. "The American Journal of Psychiatry estimates that mental illness results in lost earnings of $193.2 billion per year."(p. 35) How do lost earnings from mental illness connect to global warming? How is a person "grievously hurt by global warming?" I think liberals and environmentalists have the answer already figured out.

I do not know about you but I need to take something for my headache before a much-deserved Realityville break in order to restore my sanity. Environmental piracy activism for the sake of controlling the globe's productive population is a mental disease in itself.

Drinking Global Warming Propaganda

On a domestic flight in 2011, I was handed a bright, red and white napkin with cute polar bears on both sides with the logo, "Together We Can Help Protect Their Home." The Coca Cola famous trademark was augmented by the words, "Arctic Home."

I decided to check their Arctic Home website. It was exquisitely done, with soothing, sleep-inducing sounds of ocean waves and beautiful shots of polar bears in their Arctic habitat. The site explained, "Our goal, in partnership with the World Wildlife Fund, is to raise awareness and funds to help create a safe haven for polar bears on Arctic refuge. As a symbol of our commitment, for the first time ever, we are turning our red Coca Cola can white. Please join us by making a donation so the polar bear always has a place to call home."

Coca Cola gave up to $1 million in total donations made with a product code through March 15, 2012. It seemed like a worthy cause. However, I was not aware that the polar bears needed a safe haven on Arctic refuge, their home turf. I do not know of many people currently or in the past that have made too many tracks on Arctic refuge, deliberately trying to disrupt their home.

I do know that Al Gore made a Power Point presentation to the Nobel Prize committee, claiming that the polar bear habitat is threatened by global warming. Since bears cannot find ice floes to rest on, as ice areas are rapidly melting, polar bears were drowning. The statement was proven later to be utterly false. Bears are good swimmers, can swim long distances and melted ice refreezes. The bear population had increased five times by the last count and the video used of the melting ice caps was quite old. According to data, the caps melt and refreeze each year. It is sad that the truly deserving candidate, Irena Sendler, who saved thousands of Jewish children from the Holocaust, lost her Nobel Peace Prize to Al Gore.

Coca Cola had another related link, Live Positively.com. Under many headings such as Planet, Climate Protection, Sustainability, Water Conservation, Community Partnerships, Global Water Challenge, Sustainable Agriculture, Sustainable Packaging, Water Stewardship, Water Footprint Assessment, I was struck by the similarity of its goals and buzzwords to the goals of UN Agenda 21.

I found out that a way had been devised to measure **water footprint**. I was familiar with the hoax of measuring carbon footprint, a way to carbon tax offending corporations and enrich the coffers of governments, particularly the United Nations. The Cap and Trade legislation that failed in Congress would have made many people billionaires, including Al Gore.

The Water Stewardship and Replenish Report of January 2011 documents how the Nature Conservancy and Global Environment and Technology Foundation developed the methodologies in calculating liters of water replenished. (Community Water Partnership Reports)

Community Watershed Partnership is "working to provide safe water to primary schools in Western Kenya" and other countries.

The World Wildlife Fund, Global Water Challenge, United Nations Development Programme, the Nature Conservancy, CARE, Ocean Conservancy, the CEO Water Mandate, are NGOs (Non Governmental Organizations) trying to influence our public policy on water use and reuse without input from Congress or American voters.

Every time global organizations and companies use global governance to tell us how to live, how to be better stewards of the environment, we are losing our freedom to govern ourselves. Global governance is "The framework of rules, institutions, and practices that set limits on behavior of individuals, organizations, and companies." (Henry Lamb)

Global governance and our Constitution are at odds and they cannot co-exist. Under global governance, the governed derive their freedom from the consent of the government. Our "we the people" freedom under the U.S. Constitution is a gift from our Creator.

As the Constitution declares, "All legislative power herein granted shall be vested in a Congress of the United States which shall consist of a Senate and House of Representatives." "No legislative power is supposed to go anywhere except to the people who you, the citizens of America, elect." (Lord Monckton)

"We are also involved with the Water Footprint Network to develop standards and guidelines for water footprint accounting and to define the concept of water neutrality. In 2010, we collaborated with The Nature Conservancy to look at water footprint as a water resource management tool in a report titled Product Water Footprint Assessment. (Coca Cola website)

Since the Coca Cola site describes what steps they have taken to reduce their carbon footprint and reduce greenhouse gasses emissions, it is apparent that the myth of global warming, now renamed climate change has not died, on the contrary, it has gained track.

United Nations Secretary General, Ban Ki-moon called on world leaders at a conference in Bangladesh to collaborate on establishing a multi-billion dollar fund to combat global warming. The whole world knows that global warming is a left wing manufactured hoax. Nobody has any money to give third world nations because all developed nations are broke. Nevertheless, he wants to establish a $100 billion dollar green fund each year dedicated to help countries most affected by global warming, taming the damage caused by climate change. There are no rising sea levels and there is no increased salinity of ocean water as he claims. In his opinion, the global economic crisis should not hinder the effort to fund $100 billion each year.

Nobody disputes the fact that climate does change, and that the earth does go through periods of intense natural disasters, but it has not been proven scientifically that human behavior and activity is causing them. Scientists have demonstrated the existence of intense solar flare activity and actual global cooling, when temperatures were compared over decades.

People do care about nature, a clean environment, recycling natural resources, including water, and preserving as many of the earth's species as possible. However, Paul Watson, the co-founder of Greenpeace had said, "The data does not matter, it does not matter what is true, it only matters what people believe is true." Indeed, people believe what they are told, if repeated enough, no matter what the accurate scientific data bears.

"We are on the verge of a global transformation. All we need is the right major crisis," said David Rockefeller, the Club of Rome executive member. Judi Bari, principal organizer of Earth First provides that major crisis, the supposed human destruction of the environment. "If we do not overthrow capitalism, we do not have a chance of saving the world ecologically. I think it is possible to have an ecologically sound society under socialism. I don't think it is possible under capitalism." Having lived under communism for twenty years, I have experienced firsthand the severe air, water, and soil pollution that we experienced on a daily basis. I have also seen the dangerous smog in China during the Olympic Games.

As Lord Monckton aptly described in a recent interview for the Daily Caller, we must revisit the global warming debacle. "The environmental agenda of the hard left, socialist, fascist, communist agenda has virtually nothing to do with the environment."

The global warming debacle "lacks academic rigor, intellectual honesty, and the scientific method once the hallmark of the West." We are indebted to the unknown person at the University at East Anglia who released ten years of emails between scientists. The incorrect data drove the debate in the direction of indoctrinating the planet into the Green Monster, UN Agenda 21 plan. A massive campaign was launched to de-develop the United States.

In spite of defeating Cap and Trade, the Climate-gate scandal, cheating and malevolence of East Anglia University scientists, the global warming fallacy remains an active problem because, at the level of the states, various regional greenhouse gas initiatives are still being put in place. The governor of Maryland is trying to turn the state into a "corporate fascist state" with his Plan Maryland. California has introduced draconian measures to control the harmless trace gas carbon dioxide, necessary for all life. (Lord Monckton)

The Club of Rome, an environmental think-tank, consultants to the United Nations, shocked me with their blatantly false and outrageous statement that validated how the hard left thinks and acts.

"The common enemy of humanity is man. In search of a new enemy to unite us, we came up with the idea that pollution, the threat of global warming, water shortages, famine, and the like would fit the bill. All these dangers are caused by human intervention, and it is only through changed attitudes and behavior that they can be overcome. The real enemy then, is humanity itself."

Climate scaremongering "is nothing less than shutting down the West." If you shut down Maryland completely and return it to Stone Age, it will be extinguished or offset by three days of economic activity in China. "This global warming scare is an attempt to establish a tyranny over the mind of man. A love of nature... is something that lies very deep within all of us, and this is what the hard left is so ruthlessly and so profitably exploiting." Don't ever give money again to the Environmental Defense Fund, Greenpeace, and the Worldwide Fund, no matter how many cuddly teddy bears, panda bears, or penguins they show you." In spite of spending $3 billion on environmental propaganda, these organizations are losing the argument. (Lord Monckton)

Polar bears have nothing to fear from human activity. It is the fear mongering from the left that is problematic.

Green Energy Is Awash in Red Ink

American people are beginning to notice that the "green energy" is not so green after all, it is awash in red ink.

"Green jobs" were promised all over Europe when Spanish voters swept into power the Socialist party in 2004. More entitlements and withdrawal from the war in the Middle East were the icing on the cake. The Socialists presided initially over a period of sustained economic growth prompted by overbuilding and housing explosion. Today Spain has 5 million unemployed, a huge public debt, and the *"indignados"* (the indignants) who are a small and disruptive *minoritarios.*

Mariano Rajoy, the leader of the conservative Popular Party won the prime minister post in a landslide victory. The voters spoke loud and clear against the Socialists' lavish spending and mismanagement of the economy. Considering the severe economic problems the Spanish economy is battling, European Central Bank and the European Stability Mechanism bailouts are the only solutions to keep Spain in the European Union.

Europeans keep voting for right of center parties, but the spending spree and the "green economy" march on. According to Daniel Hannan, "only three per cent of European Union nationals have leftist governments (Austria, Denmark, Cyprus and Slovenia). Yet spending continues to rise (except on defense), bureaucracies continue to grow, powers continue to shift from national capitals to Brussels." No matter how Europeans vote, as long as Brussels dictates the laws and Germany runs the monetary policy, the "green" oligarchy rules.

On the home front, the bankrupt solar panel manufacturer Solyndra's employees qualified for **trade adjustment assistance.** After blowing $528 million dollars in taxpayer support, Solyndra's 1,100 laid off workers received $13,000 each in federal aid packages, including job retraining and income assistance.

Trade adjustment assistance was intended to ease the burden on the victims of free trade, to provide special unemployment benefits, loans, retraining programs, and other aid to workers and firms that were harmed by foreign competition after they've been in business for a while.

Solyndra was hardly in business long enough to prove that it could not compete against the Chinese who were making solar panels quite cheaply. The information was already available that the Chinese were making solar panels for $1 or less each. Now the taxpayers have to cough up another $14.3 million in federal aid as a direct result of the bankruptcy. If the workers were "highly skilled" as the Department of Energy documents show, why do they need retraining?

President Obama gave Solyndra $535 million in loan guarantees in 2009 as part of his program for "green jobs" and sang its praises at the Freemont, Ca plant. The company burned cash so quickly, that the Department of Energy had to restructure the original defaulted loan in order to help Solyndra survive. During renegotiations of the loan, private investors were placed ahead in line to receive the first $75 million recovered in the event of liquidation, clearly in violation of DOE loan rules.

Since President Obama extolled the virtues of clean solar energy, why is it that Solyndra could not make a profit in such a hot market? Was this crony capitalism or a photo opportunity for the White House to waste more taxpayer money?

Energy Secretary Steven Chu and the DOE have approved in September a $737 million loan guarantee to Tonopah Solar Energy for a 110-megawatt solar tower on federal land near Tonopah, Nevada, and a $337 million guarantee for Mesquite Solar 1 to develop a 150-megawatt solar plant near Phoenix, both under the same program as Solyndra.

If Americans have spoken loud and clear that they want drilling for oil here in order to ease the dependence on the Middle East importation, why are we still pursuing expensive solar and wind energy that cannot even begin to replace the energy currently produced by fossil fuels that our huge economy needs? Why are we not building nuclear power plants? Why did President Obama stop the Keystone XL pipeline from Canada that would have delivered crude all the way to Texas? Why does he want to bankrupt the coal industry? No matter what the majority of American voters want and no matter how they cast their ballots, the ruling power elite ignore them.

Another sector of Obama's "green economy" was in financial trouble, the renewable electricity grid. Among "smart grid" companies that had received taxpayer loans was Beacon Power that manufactured flywheel energy storage technology.

Beacon received $43 million loan guarantees from the same stimulus-funded program that financed Solyndra. Beacon filed for bankruptcy in October 2011 and announced in November 2011 that it would likely liquidate its assets instead of restructuring, meaning that the government might not recoup the $43 million through bankruptcy proceedings.

Ener1 received more than $120 million in federal grants. It was delisted by NASDAQ for failure to comply with SEC filing requirements after suffering heavy losses and firing its top executives. Other "green energy sectors" would follow.

The Smart Meter lawsuit in California would put in jeopardy the manufacturers of such meters if the judge would rule that all litigants must have their Smart Meters replaced with traditional meters. The Obama administration had already spent hundreds of millions of dollars for the deployment of Smart Meters across the country and especially in California.

A class action lawsuit in California has brought the following issues in front of the Administrative Judge Amy C. Yip-Kikugawa, who ordered PG&E, SCE, SDG&E, and Southern California Gas Company to explain Smart Meter transmission details.
- misleading representation
- public exposure to pulsing RF radiation
- UL misrepresentation
- failure to disclose smart meter defects

- misrepresentation concerning FCC guidelines
- unlawful use of customer property
- excessive conduction
- excessive RF radiation
- failure to investigate customer complaints
- Americans with Disabilities Act Violation
- customer discrimination

The "green industry" with its manufactured "green jobs," pushed by United Nations globalists who have scared and convinced billions of people that global warming is real and is the result of human activity, is a multi-trillion dollar profitable hoax. This hoax will extort huge fees in carbon emission taxes, flushing taxes, carbon footprint taxes, water footprint taxes, and other yet unnamed "green" taxes across the globe.

Billions of dollars are spent to retrofit homes, cars, plants, entire industries, products, roads, medications and hospital care, food, agricultural methods, education, travel, water access, and land access, in the name of saving the "green" planet. Every facet of human life and every human being will be better controlled by a handful of omnipotent and omniscient oligarchs.

Environmental Justice

Class warfare is about to get larger and more confusing – environmental justice will take the stage next to social justice. Executive Order 12898 signed on February 11, 1994 by President Bill Clinton set out to address environmental justice concerns in minority and low-income populations by requiring federal agencies to do the following:

- Develop an "environmental justice strategy"
- Promote enforcement of health and environmental laws in low-income and minority population areas
- Improve research and data collection in environmental justice issues
- Identify minority and low-income patterns of consumption of natural resources
- Every agency must have environmental justice as part of their mission
- Every agency must identify and address "disproportionately high and adverse human health or environmental effects of programs, policies, and activities on minority and low-income populations"

"Environmental justice as a social movement has grown rapidly since the early 1990s in response to concerns about disproportionate environmental burdens in poor, indigenous and minority communities. Natural resources and the environment played an early and important role in helping bring national attention to this emerging social and political problem." (University of Michigan, School of Natural Resources and Environment)

"Environmental Justice seeks to help the public and policymakers use scientific information to build sustainable communities world-wide," said Professor Bunyan I. Bryant Jr., coordinator of the Environmental Justice field of study.

Sustainable communities was one of the stated goals explained in the 40 chapters of the United Nations Agenda 21 document signed in1992 by 179 nations in Rio de Janeiro. "The recommendations are not legally binding but nations that signed it are morally obligated to implement them according to the United Nations."

The EPA administrator cited in a memo dated January 2010 "environmental justice as one of the agency's top priorities." EPA released its "Plan Environmental Justice 2014" in September 2011. The Plan EJ 2014 has three goals:

- To protect the environment and health in communities overburdened by pollution
- To empower communities to take action to improve their health and environment
- To establish partnerships with local, state, tribal, federal governments, and organizations to achieve healthy and sustainable communities.

The third goal is worrisome as it expands the EPA's control over our lives in order to achieve the UN Agenda 21's goal of sustainable communities. It is unclear how they are going to measure scientifically which communities are "overburdened by pollution" or how income correlates to air, water, or soil pollution intake by people with lower incomes since we all breathe the same air, eat food grown from the same soil, and drink water from the same sources. As this is a social movement invented by the leftist and Marxist elements in our society, aided by the interests of UN Agenda 21, it hardly represents a scientific endeavor.

U.S. Government Accountability Office (GAO) was asked to examine the EPA's environmental justice, "the fair treatment and meaningful involvement of all people in developing, implementing and enforcing environmental laws, regulations, and policies," and published its report in October 2011. A draft of GAO's report was provided to the EPA. EPA disagreed with two of GAO's recommendations, partially agreed with one recommendation, and did not address the remaining recommendations.

The Council on Environmental Quality oversees the federal government's compliance with Executive Order 12898 and with the National Environmental Policy Act (NEPA). NEPA was enacted by Congress in 1970 to "assure for all Americans safe, healthful, productive, and aesthetically and culturally pleasing surroundings." Congress also mandated that, "before federal agencies undertake a major federal action significantly affecting the environment, they must consider the environmental impact of such actions on the quality of the human environment, such as cultural, economic, social, or health effects including those on populations and areas with environmental justice concerns."

Plan EJ 2014 advances environmental justice by:

- Rulemaking (Writers must include environmental justice in their plans.)
- Permitting (EPA-issued permits to address environmental pollution on poor populations)
- Compliance and Enforcement (Targeting pollution problems in disadvantaged communities)
- Community-based action (Giving grants and technical assistance to overburdened communities to help address environmental problems)
- Administration-wide action on environmental justice ("Establishing partnerships and initiatives with other federal agencies to support holistic approaches to addressing environmental, social, and economic burdens of affected communities.")

I was confused since EPA stated that they wanted to apply Environmental Justice scientifically, but the language changes to "holistic." Is this another effort by EPA to control our population, land, air, and water under the guise of giving help to disadvantaged populations, a form of spreading the wealth through one more social program?

The stakeholders of the environmental justice plan are identified as the National Environmental Justice Advisory Council, the Federal

Interagency Working Group on Environmental Justice, state agencies, and community groups.

The EPA relies on the Clean Air Act and the Resource Conservation and Recovery Act to implement its programs. If a state is approved by EPA as meeting relevant criteria, the state is responsible to monitor and give permits, thus becoming a primary enforcer. States thus become responsible to carry out EPA's environmental justice plan.

The EPA has national ambient air quality standards for certain pollutants that are harmful to the public and the environment. State Implementation Plans must carry out these standards. Grants and loans programs such as Clean Water and Drinking Water State Revolving Funds must now include Environmental Justice in their plans and programs. States, identified as key stakeholders, received limited and insufficient details about the incorporation of environmental justice into their plans.

According to the GAO report released October 2011, EPA's Plan EJ 2014 provides limited detail to states about their role in ongoing planning or about the states' role in a nationally consistent environmental justice-screening tool (EJ SCREEN). The report points out the lack of standard definitions for basic environmental justice terms, such as minority and low-income.

The EPA responded that it did not develop terms on purpose because it did not want to leave out certain communities that did not fit their predetermined definition. In other words, environmental justice will not be just at all, it will be capricious, random, and it will not be scientific.

Community groups will buy into the Environmental Justice idea through funding mechanisms, training, technical assistance, and environmental indoctrination.

Environmental Justice will become further pandering to low-income voters, redistribution of wealth, control of natural resources, economic activity, land, and water use, expanding UN Agenda 21's goals.

Food Justice

"Food is one of the only base human needs where the American government lets the private market dictate its delivery to our communities." This is how Tracie McMillan described the capitalist food distribution in the U.S., the number one exporter of corn and wheat to the rest of the world. McMillan is a political science major who wrote a book on nutrition entitled, "The American Way of Eating."

McMillan decried the fact that our free market decides food delivery. She emphasized that, unless government controls food delivery and supply, food injustice will continue to dominate this country. She assumed, "Expensive food that took time to prepare, wasn't for people like us," meaning blue-collar families.

As a mom and wife, I disagree. Food that takes time to prepare is cheaper than any boxed meals bought in the grocery store. Potato chips and other snacks, ounce per ounce, are also more expensive than nutritious foods prepared at home. The ingredients may seem more expensive initially, but the quantity prepared in the end is larger and feeds more people, allowing for refrigeration and freezing for later use. The price per meal is thus cheaper than any fast food or prefabricated food.

According to McMillan, average Americans are denied good and fresh food. The statement is disingenuous because poor families receive electronic food benefits cards, formerly known as food stamps. Currently, 43 million Americans are on food stamps, the highest number in any administration. Additionally, their children receive 2-3 free meals at school.

First Lady Michelle Obama spearheaded the effort to make school lunches nutritious and low-caloric. The Agriculture Secretary Tom Vilsack translated her directives into the 2010 "Healthy and Hunger-Free Kids Act," a one-size fits all national school diet, because some kids are overweight. Kindergartners through fifth grade can have up to 650 calories, sixth through eighth graders can have 700 calories, and high school students can only have 850 calories. This sounds healthy unless you are a high school athlete who burns 2,000-3,000 calories per day during practice.

Rep. Steve King has introduced legislation to repeal the new rules. The new guidelines of the nanny state were characterized by the co-sponsor of the bill, Rep. Tim Huelskamp of Kansas, as a "perfect example of what is wrong with government: misguided inputs, tremendous waste, and unaccomplished goals."

There is nothing in the world that prevents any American, rich or poor, from purchasing fresh ingredients in order to prepare wholesome foods. Nobody twists their arms to buy potato chips, beer, candy, and boxed meals that are not as healthy as meals prepared at home. The average American household spends 15 percent of their income on food, one of the lowest percentages in the developed world.

The ultimate liberal goal is not a fair distribution of fresh food. The market distributes goods according to supply and demand and manufacturers distribute their products according to demand. The intent is to take away our freedoms. Food is now a variable of socialist class struggle and a form of discrimination because "the poor and downtrodden are getting junk food while the snobs get fancy food."

According to food police at school, your mom does not know what is best for you, your government does, following Michelle Obama's nutrition dictates. Food and the distribution of food has become a social issue in the collectivist/socialist ideology. We must all be equal in the leftist view and the government must step in to regulate food distribution and delivery.

"Average, ordinary Americans, the 99 percent, are denied expensive food that takes time to prepare." McMillan "stares at America's bounty, noting that so few seem able to share in it fully and she asks: 'What would it take for us all to eat well?'" (Rush Limbaugh)

"Food is one of the only base human needs where the American government lets the private market dictate its delivery to our communities." Tracie McMillan is thus saying, "Capitalism and the private sector are discriminating against the average, ordinary American by not delivering him quality food." Perhaps bringing in government food agents to check children's boxed lunches in school as it happened in North Carolina would solve the quandary of proper food delivery and nutrition.

I should tell McMillan about basic economics, the price mechanism that assigns the highest prices to the goods in greatest demand and then allows individual consumers to pursue their own self-interests. Price acts as a rationing device. Available supplies are distributed to match different consumer preferences as well as possible. If a centrally planned economy, socialist or communist, rations food by distributing the same amount to everyone, then everybody ends up with less of everything, sometimes experiencing severe shortages. The price system or the capitalist system allows each consumer to set his or her own priorities. If the left wants equality, then efficiency goes out the window.

Central government planning under socialism/communism was so bad that we were issued rationing coupons and a black market emerged. People were hoarding food, selling it at scalping prices, stealing coupons, or trading them for other services. When we ran out of rationing coupons, we could not buy certain foods. Government did not know best, it created chronic shortages of food, starvation, and a depressed and gaunt population, fighting in long lines on a daily basis for the last liter of milk, loaf of bread, bones stripped of meat, pat of butter, pound of flour or sugar, liter of oil, or kilo of shriveled potatoes. The population was indeed lean, skin and bones, with atrophied muscles from lack of protein, and vitamin deficient.

The capitalist economy allocates resources well - what to produce, how to produce it, and how to distribute the resulting goods, without any central direction from the government or concern for the public interest. Socialists/communists have predicted that such unplanned system would result in chaos. However, the socialist/communist economies degenerated into dismal failures and were rejected by the people while the capitalist economic system thrived. Even Karl Marx admitted," Capitalism is the most powerful mode of production available."

The price mechanism or Adam Smith's "invisible hand" always ranks potential consumers of food in the order of the intensity of their preference for that food, as indicated by the amount they are willing to spend on it.

The logic of Economics 101 flies in the face of the left and its newest "food justice" platform. The left never lets logic deter them from their true agenda, taking away our freedoms to choose, installing social justice, environmental justice, food justice, and completing the radical transformation of America into Fabian Socialism.

Making Eco-Village with Green Mansions

Loudon County, Virginia, is one of the richest counties in the nation. They are at the forefront of implementing the environmentalist green agenda of living in an eco-village. The residents are "a typical middle class mix of mostly white-collar workers." (Washington Post, December 31, 2011)

If we consider this group typical middle-class, we should consider the price of homes in this utopian "paradise." The last home bought in this Shangri-La in September 2011, a foreclosed home, cost $359,000. Some sell between $895,000 and $1.7 million.

The roads are unpaved, the terrain is rough, and the non-existent lawns are typical of wilderness grasses. The inhabitants like to keep them this way in order to reduce their carbon footprint. The gravel roads and the untended surroundings are definitely intentional.

"The development attracts a self-selecting group of people who, to varying degrees, are in search of a more sustainable and locally-centered lifestyle." This may sound admirable to some people, but it regurgitates the buzzwords and goals listed in the UN Agenda 21. I am not sure about you, but I like my roads paved. They are so much gentler on my car and more pleasant to travel on.

Gravel is used to reduce harmful runoff into the Potomac River and to slow down auto traffic. Parking is delineated to lots around the commune, not in front of people's homes.

According to Washington Post, "although it's become almost mainstream to be 'green,' residents of Eco-Village, founded in 1996, are on the cutting edge of the movement."

I am unsure how mainstream United Nations green growth dictates are in America. I do know that most Americans do not desire to live such "locally centered lifestyles." We love our cars, we love our roads, our cities, and we are not so much fond of village life, which most societies try to escape. We would like to be able to keep our mobility and freedom to go greater distances in search of the American dream. Trying to fashion 19th century lifestyles for the rest of us in the 21st century is not exactly the majority of Americans' idea of progress.

Residents, in communist fashion, must abide by strict ecological standards for building, lighting, and landscaping. Perhaps they should include goats in their lawn management program. "Villagers" can only pick from six approved house plans and must build in clusters of one-third to three-quarter acre lots for a total of 14 houses. There are 14 more lots, nine of which were vacant and for sale at $80,000 a piece. How many middle-class Americans can afford to pay $80,000 for such a tiny piece of land?

"Eco-Villagers" planted 11,000 trees in order to replace flora with indigenous varieties. After all, according to National Geographic, any species of flora that are not local represents "biological imperialism." Planting trees is a laudable effort; it makes the area a "heaven for birds," which prompted the Audubon Society to name the Eco-Village a Home Wildlife Sanctuary. "Eighty-five percent of its 90 acres are protected open space." This brings to mind the Biodiversity Plan of UN Agenda 21 which aims to make most land protected and unavailable to human use.

The founders of the village lived since 2001 in a "straw bale house with timber beams, encased in thick stucco walls." I remember living in my grandma's straw and mud house in the early sixties in communist Romania. It was a heaven for mice and rats who tunneled and made their homes inside the walls. We could hear busy rat stomping feet all night long.

A solar system on the roof of a typical Eco-Village home heats the house with a complicated system of pipes and switches and an electric backup, just in case the sun does not shine at all. Some homes have geothermal underground pipes and windows are strategically placed to capture more sun.

"Eco-Villagers" claim that their choices have not been about the money, implying that the costs were not effective. They are well-off people trying to escape "the traffic and congestion of Vienna," an upscale town with homes in the millions of dollars.

Potluck suppers and tree planting parties are the life of the "village." Adults and children are required to do monthly community service in the Eco-Village commune. It reminds me of our forced "volunteer" work we had to do in the communist dictatorship in Romania – 30 days in the fall, picking the crops, and 30 days in the spring, planting the crops. We were not given as much as water during the 10 hours of daily forced labor.

Americans care for their environment and have plans in place for tree planting in order to prevent deforestation. We do not wish to excessively pollute our environment and do our part to protect it. The capitalist free market does a good job of eliminating and weeding out companies who over-pollute. The price system, Adam Smith's "invisible hand," intervenes magically to price out and drive out polluters.

EPA rules and regulations protect our soil, water, and air. We do not need to revert to medieval times of village living in order to protect the planet.

The ecological "green" promoters have planned huge economic gains from carbon footprint taxes. Cap and trade has been defeated so far yet the United Nations, supported by the Sierra Club and other NGOs, successfully passed carbon footprint taxes in Europe and in the wonderful state of California.

President Obama's Energy Policy

The President exhibited incredible callousness and total disconnect from the plight of the American people when he advised a young man who was lamenting the high price of gasoline, to trade in his gas-guzzler SUV for a better mileage car made by GM or Ford. It was eerie to see someone so detached from the very policies that he implemented.

Gas has doubled in price since Obama became President, in part due to his disastrous economic policies that favor foreign interests while hurting national interests, particularly the seven year moratorium he imposed on oil drilling in the Gulf of Mexico.

Gas prices escalated in Europe to $9-$10 a gallon in some EU countries. Gas prices are a reflection of the weak dollar and high taxes. Gas prices are quoted in petrodollars as per an international convention signed long time ago in New Hampshire. Diesel used to be cheaper in Europe but it is now on par with gasoline. Ever conscious environmental pirates have produced a new brand of Diesel, Diesel Maxx, a mixture of Diesel and biofuels such as rapeseed oil in Romania. This Diesel Maxx was more expensive than regular Diesel and priced around $11 per gallon in October 2012.

The compliant media is suddenly mum about the rapid escalating oil prices. The same media came unhinged when gas prices hit $4 per gallon under President George W. Bush and criticized him at nauseam. California's gas prices have reached $6.59 per gallon in some areas by October 2012 and Governor Brown was considering relaxing the very stringent regulations in refining crude oil which increase the cost of gasoline to such expensive levels.

The President appears detached from reality, as if it is someone else's job to make sure the American people's economic interests are preserved and protected and he is just an outside witness and observer in perennial campaign mode.

President Obama seems to be the number one cheerleader for world energy interests, the United Nations' "green" agenda and especially third world dictatorships; he presents himself as the global president. America is a pebble in his shoe, which he dismisses with a flick of his foot. Every day he chops off another branch while the tree of liberty is bleeding heavily.

Energy generated by oil, natural gas, and coal has been the lifeblood of this economy for generations. One of the first wells that produced oil, which was marketed, was drilled near Marietta, Ohio in 1814.

The inventions of the combustion engine in 1895 and Henry Ford's first motorcar in 1896 were the beginning of America's love affair with gasoline, cars, the wide-open roads, and constant mobility.

World War I (1914-1918) was the first conflict where control of the oil supply was important for tanks, ships, and airplanes.

Oil was discovered in Bahrain in 1932 and Saudi Arabia granted oil concessions to Standard Oil of California in 1933. In 1938, oil was discovered in Kuwait and Saudi Arabia. The supply of the Middle East oil started during this period.

During World War II (1939-1945), the control of the oil supply from the Middle East and Baku, Russia, played a large role in the events of the war and the ultimate victory of the allies. The allies bombed heavily the refineries in Ploiesti, Romania that supplied gasoline to the German army. Even Japan was weakened in the latter part of the war by having its oil supply cut off.

In 1960, the Organization of Petroleum Exporting Countries (OPEC) was founded in Baghdad by Saudi Arabia, Venezuela, Kuwait, Iraq, and Iran. Current members are Algeria, Indonesia, Iran, Iraq, Kuwait, Libya, Nigeria, Qatar, Saudi Arabia, United Arab Emirates, and Venezuela.

As the U.S. economy grew, we became more and more dependent on our cars, on transportation of goods, parts, and food via eighteen-wheelers, airplanes, and large trucks. To deny the fact that the fate of our economy does not rest on fossil fuels would be delusional. Wind and solar energy cannot provide the energy necessary to run our economy at a reasonable price. Nuclear energy provides much needed supply but the recent disaster in Japan has made regulators even wearier of new reactors.

We have been told for a long time that oil is a fossil fuel produced by decaying dinosaurs. Environmentalists have led us to believe that the decaying fauna and flora produced "the black gold" of which there is a limited supply. The truth is that German scientists during World War II discovered the Fischer-Tropsch process, allowing them to form synthetic hydrocarbons. Dr. Thomas Gold talked about oil as an "abiotic" natural product of the earth, produced at very deep levels where there are no animals or plants. (Thomas Gold, "The Deep Hot Biosphere: The Myth of Fossil Fuels")

Crony capitalists who received billions in mandatory taxpayer-funded subsidies to produce expensive wind, solar, and biofuels at the expense of the food supply and higher prices and financial burden to taxpayers had no interest to drill for cheaper sources. Cronies were happy to waste billions in taxpayer dollars and President Obama cheered them on, continuing to throw money to bankrupted "renewable energy" enterprises, at least 12 so far.

New regulations by the Environmental Protection Agency and the Department of Energy have cost more than $100 million each to implement. Total regulatory costs from all departments increased from $1,172 trillion in 2009 to $1,752 trillion in 2012. (American Energy Alliance).

The oil industry is not interested in producing more expensive synthetic oil because they can drill for cheaper oil in the ground or extract it through "fracking" and "oil/kerogen shale." The Bakken shale reserves in North Dakota and Montana are expected to double output to about 1.2 million barrels per day by 2015. (Reuters, September 20, 2012)

The Department of Energy said that "there are more proven crude oil reserves worldwide than ever in recorded history, despite the fact that worldwide consumption of crude oil has doubled since the 1970s."(Energy Information Administration of U.S. Department of Energy)

The very liberals who have pushed so hard for wind energy are now driving to stop their use in many areas because of the unbearable noise level, bird kills, and unsightly appearance. Areas in

California have passed laws to turn windmills off when the wind surpasses 23 mph. The problem is that windmills operate most efficiently when winds are 30 mph and higher. Turning them off at 23 mph winds is a losing proposition, causing townships to lose millions of dollars annually that they have invested in the mills infrastructure.

After higher oil prices in the seventies, we have switched from large gas-guzzlers to smaller, more energy-efficient cars and trucks. We even converted engines to natural gas for a while in the early 1980s. As soon as the embargo was lifted and the oil was plentiful, we started driving big SUVs, larger trucks, and vans.

Americans prefer to drive SUVs because they are safer vehicles now than they were when they were first brought to the market, and are safer than cars. Nobody wants to buy the Chevy Volt; GM has only sold a few thousands to the most dedicated environmentalists. To drive Americans to buy the Volt, the government even tried to impose an additional 50 cents per gallon gas tax. The Volt is an expensive toy that goes 20 miles before it needs a full recharge. And Tesla, a more expensive, luxury electric car, "bricks" itself if the charge drains completely, requiring a very expensive factory engine rebuild costing $40,000 plus.

Because OPEC is a monopoly and colludes overtly through production quotas, the price of oil can be driven up and down by simply having a meeting and deciding the direction prices should go, and adjusting production accordingly.

The oil futures speculators can also influence prices based on world unrest, civil strife, lack of confidence in the market, and government insecurity in general. To make matters worse, we can only refine so much oil at one time since no additional refineries have been built in years.

The worst variable that affects the price of oil is the value of the dollar itself because the price of oil is quoted in dollars. Banks keep accounting outside of the U.S. of "petrodollars" money stock. When the dollar is weak, the price per barrel escalates. Venezuela's Hugo Chavez tried to change the quoting of oil prices from dollar to euro unsuccessfully.

President Obama had stated that his goal was to drive coal plants into bankruptcy and energy costs under his presidency would necessarily skyrocket. I am not sure his supporters understand that their "green" Priuses need gasoline and Volts need electricity generated by coal plants. We do not have enough nuclear power or hydro-generated electricity.

Finally, the delicate balance of supply and demand is very important as it can drive up the price of oil immediately if there is a real or perceived diminished supply. Ban the domestic drilling for oil for seven years as President Obama did in the Gulf of Mexico, and you have a formula for very high prices at the pump.

Ironically, the President gave Petrobras of Brazil $2 billion of U.S. taxpayer dollars to drill for oil in the Gulf of Mexico, practically in our own back yard. He assured them that the U.S. would be their "best customer." It turns out that China is their main customer. Could it be because Soros has again a controlling interest in Petrobras? Why can we not drill for our own oil? Many other countries are drilling in the Gulf of Mexico such as China, Russia, Venezuela, U.K., to name just a few.

Should our American President have said no to the Keystone XL pipeline that would have brought much needed oil from Canada to be refined in the U.S., thus reducing our oil supply dependency on the Middle East? Should we not exploit the abundant shale reserves in the United States?

The Middle East is exploding in an orgy of Muslim Brotherhood and Al Qaeda terrorist takeover attacks, thanks to the help of our administration's insane apologetic foreign policy aimed to appease terrorists while ignoring allies, and removing from power dictators like Mubarak of Egypt and Gadhafi of Libya who have kept terrorist pockets and rebellious tribes in their countries in check for forty years. How expensive would the Middle East oil become in the face of unrest all over the Muslim world, fighting, burning, killing of our Ambassador in Benghazi and three other Americans in the Middle East while the U.S. apologized to Jihadis whose sensibilities have been presumably "insulted" by a movie trailer nobody had seen on YouTube? Exporting democracy to countries that follow a seventh century theocratic doctrine, ideology, and religion does not work.

Even worse, we are exporting gasoline to Hugo Chavez's Venezuela because he has neglected to build refineries in his communist centrally-planned economy and thus Venezuela does not have enough refining capacity for their abundant oil resources.

Is this the schizophrenic policy and advice a President should give his own citizens, get used to high gas prices or switch to an electric or hybrid car? Should he not implement a viable energy policy that benefits the economy and does not impoverish its citizens who have to decide whether they are going to buy expensive gas to go to work or buy expensive food trucked in by Diesel "guzzling" eighteen-wheelers?

The Non-Energy Generating Department of Energy and the Smart Grid

If you ask Americans what the Department of Energy does, the majority will tell you, they are tasked with generating electricity and other forms of energy. The real mission of the DOE is quite different.

The Department of Energy was formed after the oil crisis on August 8, 1977 by Jimmy Carter who signed **The Department of Energy Organization Act of 1977.** It began operations on October 1, 1977. The DOE operates 34 science laboratories.

As part of the $789 billion economic stimulus package in the **American Recovery and Reinvestment Act of 2009**, Congress provided DOE with an additional $38.3 billion for fiscal years 2009 and 2010, adding about 75 percent to Energy's annual budgets. Most of the stimulus spending was in the form of grants and contracts.

According to their website, "The Department of Energy is the single largest Federal government supporter of basic research in the physical sciences in the United States, providing more than 40 percent of total Federal funding for this vital area of national importance. It oversees, and is the principal Federal funding agency of the Nation's research programs in high-energy physics, nuclear physics, and fusion energy sciences. Such a diverse research portfolio supports tens of thousands of principal investigators, post-doctoral students, and graduate students who are tackling some of the most challenging scientific questions of our era."

I would like to translate this into simpler English; the Department of Energy does not generate directly or indirectly one watt of electricity. Under **Science and Technology**, the DOE spends our tax dollars, on pure research:

Research and Development

"DOE manages fundamental research programs in basic energy sciences, biological and environmental sciences, and computational science and is the Federal Government's largest single provider of funds for materials and chemical sciences."

Ensuring the supply of radio isotopes

"Radio Isotopes have become key agents in the diagnosis and effective treatment of various cancers, heart disease and other medical problems. DOE programs ensure the availability of an adequate supply of medical and research isotopes, which is essential to the Nation's health care system." Like most Americans, I was unaware that the DOE is concerned with our health and medical research.

Research in environmental sciences

"The Department conducts research in climate change, geophysics, genomics, life sciences, and science education, as well as scientific research in the areas of fossil energy and environmental science." This is strange since EPA concerns itself with these very same issues.

A diverse research portfolio

"DOE sponsors research at universities located in 49 states, Puerto Rico and the District of Columbia. These efforts support tens of thousands of principal investigators, post-doctoral students, and graduate students who are tackling some of the most challenging scientific questions of our era." This is fine, but is it the job of the Department of Energy to provide grant money for university research?

The DOE is interested in the "consequences of energy production, development, and use, investing in basic research on global climate change and environmental remediation." I thought Al Gore's global warming schemes have been debunked long time ago. His Nobel Peace Prize for the Power Point Presentation should have been rescinded.

Few people know that the DOE has founded and plays an important role in the Human Genome Project in 1986 and "invests in basic research on global climate change and environmental remediation."

Microbe research "will play an important role in helping solve DOE's mission challenges in energy production and environmental cleanup." How is that possible to have a mission challenge of energy production when you are not producing one watt of electricity, you are just a bureaucrat headquartered in Washington, D.C.?

Carbon sequestration is another research mission of the DOE "to reduce the buildup of greenhouse gases in the atmosphere." The Department of Energy "strives to deliver fundamental knowledge of biological systems that can be used to address DOE needs in clean energy, carbon sequestration, and environmental cleanup." How does the DOE have needs in clean energy, carbon sequestration, and environmental clean up? Is the EPA not tasked with environmental cleanup? Does the free market not decide the needs in energy? Now, all of a sudden, by fiat, the DOE is going to decide our needs (demand) for energy by forcing the installation of Smart Meters into our homes? Obviously, the DOE does not supply energy at all.

Smart Meters are digital electricity consumption readers that are installed under the guise that the old ones are either cracked or not reading properly. Most people acquiesce, without realizing that they have just allowed the installation of a personal surveillance device.

This device will tell a distant data server to whom they do not have access, how many watts they consume, when they turn off and on every lamp in their home, how many computers they have, electric gadgets, when they sleep, when they are on vacation, when they are not home, their living pattern in general, basically a search of their life and home without a warrant.

The information recorded can and will be sold to anyone who is willing to pay. Pirates can intercept the wireless signal and constant data streaming from your home. The one-watt licensed by the FCC device will aid and abet the punishing of people for doing things in the privacy of their own homes, big brother watching all the time. Furthermore, electricity can be cut off from a remote location during peak usage time, middle of summer and middle of winter.

Tapping into someone's home is illegal in all 50 states and federal territories. The DOE affiliates use "implied consent" when they change the meter. People should be aware and send notices that they do not wish to have their meters changed, the old ones work just fine.

The energy sources listed by the DOE are wind, solar, renewables, oil, nuclear, natural gas, hydropower, hydrogen, geothermal, fusion, fossil fuels, electric power, coal, and bioenergy. Yet the DOE focus is on "clean fuel initiatives" none of which are cheap or cheaper than fossil fuels.

In modernizing our energy infrastructure, think Smart Grid, the focus is on our "planet's environment." Limiting environmental impact, "advances in wind, hydro and geothermal energy allow us to take advantage of clean, abundant energy." Has anybody seen cheap and abundant energy coming from wind mills or geothermal? I do know that California is turning theirs off when winds are higher than 23 mph because they are so noisy, yet windmills work best in winds 30 mph and higher.

The DOE seems preoccupied with "establishing the safety, reliability, and efficiency of energy supplies in a global marketplace." There seems to be almost an obsession with coordination with the global environment and Agenda 21 stewardship as if we already live under a one-world government of the United Nations.

Under **Energy Efficiency**, the DOE wants to protect the environment, reduce carbon emissions, and spread the wealth through the **Weatherization Assistance Program** by making the homes of "disadvantaged" more energy efficient. All of a sudden, the 47 percent of our population that pays no income taxes have become "disadvantaged" and are in dire need of assistance at every level possible at the expense of the tax-paying, hard-working middle class.

The DOE recommends that every American needs to learn how to make every day **Earth Day** and save money and energy at home by using mercury-laden, energy-saving bulbs. It does not matter that it takes 30 minutes to dispose of such broken bulbs or that they explode from time to time, sending toxic mercury throughout the house, and requiring temporary evacuation of the premises. Thomas

Edison would be turning over in his grave for the disservice they are doing to his incandescent bulb.

The DOE must protect the environment by disposing of nuclear waste properly, safely storing radioactive waste, and protecting the environment and the public. Should this not be the job of the EPA? Is this not a duplication and waste of taxpayer dollars?

The Department of Energy also provides prices and trends in areas such as petroleum, gasoline, 18-month forecast on oil, gas prices and supply, historical energy data from 1949-2004, and a primer on gasoline prices. All of this information can be obtained from other sources.

Under **National Security**, the DOE claims that it provides "cyber security protection, operations security, and prevents the spread of weapons of mass destruction." I am sure, all of us can sleep better, knowing that the Department of Energy is in control of our national security.

Finally yet importantly, "the safety of our workers and the environmental responsibility to safeguard our natural surroundings are integrated management practices throughout DOE." I may be mistaken but I thought that is why we had OSHA and the EPA.

The $29.5 billion DOE funding includes a 12 percent increase over the 2010 enacted levels. Clean energy, nuclear security, research and development are priority areas. "Savings are achieved through cuts to inefficient fossil energy programs."New grid technologies and systems will help Smart Grid and improve energy transmission efficiency."

Baltimore Gas & Electric (BGE) was denied an application by the Maryland Public Service Commission on June 22, 2010 to deploy smart grid infrastructure because it is cost effective or serves the public interest. A customer surcharge would have appeared on the bill even before the infrastructure was in place. Nobody seemed to address the issue of invasion of personal liberty and the illegality of tapping into someone's life without a warrant.

Ten states are leading the national effort to deploy the smart grid. They have been awarded 42 percent, or $1.9 billion, of the $4.5 billion earmarked for the smart grid in the stimulus named **the American Recovery and Reinvestment Act of 2009**. According to Greentech Media Research, these states are "laying the groundwork for market development of the smart grid."

- California ($303.4 million)
- Colorado ($24.1 million)
- Florida ($467.2 million)
- Massachusetts ($28.29 million)
- New Jersey ($212.4 million)
- New York ($232.2 million)
- North Carolina ($403.5 million)
- Ohio ($142.4 million)
- Pennsylvania ($466.3 million)
- Texas ($285.6 million)

About 5 percent of Americans were equipped with some form of smart grid technology by the end of 2009. That number was forecast to increase ten-fold over the next five years.

In accordance with the President's agreement at the G-20 summit in Pittsburgh, fossil fuel tax subsidies will be phased out for fossil fuel producers so that we can "transition to a 21st century energy economy."

DOE will "unleash a clean energy revolution" and "educate the next generation with 21st century skills and create a world-class workforce." I thought we did have an excellent workforce; we just lack the jobs Obama promised. Would that energy economy involve involuntary black-outs since a lot of our electricity is produced with fossil fuels?

The Department of Energy is an arm of the federal government, run by career bureaucrats who march in synch with United Nation's Agenda 21 goals of "sustainability," does not produce any energy, subsidizes for profit university and laboratory research with our taxpayer dollars, and wants to implement smart grid technology in order to control 24/7 our daily lives. Is it a good idea to allow them into our homes to install Smart Meters?

Smart Growth Plans and ICLEI

An article in the liberal Washington Post appeared with the innocuous title, "What we need: Smarter growth plans." The author was Roger K. Lewis, a practicing architect and professor emeritus at the University of Maryland. Who could possibly object to "smarter growth plans?" Except that "smart growth plans" is the euphemism used by the United Nations for its Agenda 21, a direct assault on private property rights and American sovereignty.

Roger K. Lewis suggested that "smart growth" was designed by market forces driven by "green building." He made no mention of UN Agenda 21 and ICLEI objectives and intrusion into our society since the early 1970s or the agreement signed in 1992 that went under the radar of the American people's understanding of the complex negative ramifications for our economy and our liberties.

I have not met Americans who think, "sprawl-producing planning, zoning and mortgage templates are obsolete" as the author claimed. Would Americans willingly give up their land and homes with or without compensation in exchange for a move to a densely populated high-rise, with no parking garages, no access to cars, like rats fenced in a grey concrete maze?

Communist "social engineering" that I experienced confiscated land and homes for agriculture. People were forced to move into many-storied, tiny cinder block apartments without any compensation for the land or homes bulldozed. They were forced to commute by bicycles or rickety public transit.

Lewis described subdivision developments with low-density, detached, single-family homes as outdated. He called the areas educationally dysfunctional and unsafe. American suburbia was built, he said, on four assumptions that have lost validity today:

- Unlimited supply of land
- Inexpensive and inexhaustible supply of oil
- Homogenous land use
- The American dream to own and inhabit a mortgaged house.

I am not sure how Mr. Lewis arrived at his conclusions, but we have huge domestic oil reserves if permits were issued to drill. We also have a vast land mass. Some areas have 70 or less inhabitants per square mile. Americans still want to own their own homes and want to live in a homogeneous community of other homeowners. Just because power-hungry bureaucrats at the United Nations have decided to "preserve" land and the environment for the future of the planet and its animals, neglecting the future of humans, does not mean Americans agree to this vision.

"Much of America's land cannot and should not be developed." Who has made that decision for the American people and why? Last time I checked we were free people who determined their own life choices.

"Dependency on oil and limitless use of cars pose daunting environmental, economic, and geopolitical problems." Who is going to decide the limit to our car use? Is it going to be done by law, more regulations, or executive order?

A handful of environmentalists, the EPA, and the United Nation's dictators, using faulty debunked data from the University of East Anglia or phony research are trying to separate Americans from their land use, cars, trucks, and the open-wide roads.

Lewis continued his Agenda 21 fallacy. "The traditional nuclear family – mom, dad, two to three kids and one or two pets – is now a minority of America's households." I am positive that this man was not describing America that I know and see every day. The next statement described an even more bizarre America, "Today a majority of households are people, young or old, living alone, couples or sets of unrelated individuals of various ethnicities, ages and tastes."

Lewis suggested building high-rises in "designated areas within municipalities where new development and re-development is feasible and desirable." Affordable housing is a priority and so are environmental standards. I am sure the UN agreed with him but most Americans disagree because they prefer to live in various areas, it is their choice, not the government's.

It was obvious that UN Agenda 21's "smart growth plans" will affect our future choices in how we live and where. EPA will be involved and will twist the arms of those who do not adopt such "smart growth plans," denying grants to states and cities and levying other penalties. By the time Americans realize the implications of "smart growth," they will lose their homes and lands with no compensation. At least most people who lost property under Eminent Domain have been compensated.

The International Council for Local Environmental Initiatives (ICLEI) is a conglomerate of 600 national, regional, and local government associations who promote "sustainable development" and protection of the environment because of man-made global warming that does not exist.

"Sustainable development" is the United Nations effort to contain and limit economic development in developed countries and thus control population growth. It is "sustainable de-growth," plain and simple. The focus is "low-income agriculture" and setting limits on the developed world. There are four tiers to UN's "sustainable development" plan:
- Environmental sustainability
- Economic sustainability
- Socio-political sustainability
- Cultural diversity

United Nations and its affiliates believe that first world countries polluted significantly during their development while urging third world countries to reduce pollution thus impeding their growth. Implementation of "sustainable development" would revert our society to a pre-modern lifestyle while punishing us for past transgressions that supposedly stunted the growth of other economies.

ICLEI wants to keep the environment as pristine as possible through "ideal-seeking behavior." These euphemisms are not clearly defined in terms of what or who will evaluate or set the standards for this "ideal-seeking behavior," but it does conjure up pictures of totalitarian control.

UN Agenda 21 sets up the global infrastructure to manage, count, and control assets. It is not concerned with protecting the environment or the world's resources. Agenda 21 wants change from old sector-centered ways of doing business to new approaches. The "desired future state" should be to pursue "economic prosperity, environmental quality, and social equity."

"Social equity" is an economic euphemism for "social justice," the Marxists' excuse for re-distribution of wealth to third world countries. Who gave them the authority and the mandate to initiate such a fundamental change involving transfer of property and wealth? The American people who are producers were not asked through a referendum whether we wanted our way of life to be fundamentally altered according to mandates set up by the United Nations.

In 2001 UNESCO stated in The Universal Declaration on Cultural Diversity that cultural diversity is as important as biodiversity in the sense of a more satisfactory, intellectual, emotional, moral, and spiritual existence. We are culturally diverse in the U.S. but we are Americans at the end of the day. Promoting multi-culturalism has been a disaster in Europe and resulted in the Islamification of many western countries who have lost their roots, their faith, their national pride, history, and cultural identity. It is frightening to see what some enlightened European cities have become – sewers of 7th century sectarian Islam. Who will decide the level and quality of the population's satisfaction, intellectual, emotional, moral, and spiritual existence? "Human needs must be met while preserving the environment for the future." Will the United Nations' ruling elites decide what our needs are in order to preserve the future?

ICLEI attended a United Nations conference in Nairobi, Kenya in February 2011 as representative of the interests of local governments. "In collaboration with partners such as UN-Habitat, Cities Alliance and ICLEI, UNEP (United Nations Environmental Protection) is working to make cities more livable, better prepared for the multiple environmental challenges they are facing, as well as giving them a stronger voice in the international climate negotiations." Last time I checked, global warming has been debunked as a hoax and UN rapidly changed its name to climate change, continuing the attempt to fleece developed countries. Most importantly, ICLEI cannot represent our local governments because it is a violation of our Constitution.

In October 2009 in Bangkok, ICLEI stated, 'local governments are offering national governments our partnership in the fight against climate change." ICLEI wants local governments to collaborate with national governments to fight against climate change, the very change that has been scientifically debunked.

Article I, Section 10 of the Constitution states clearly, "No State shall enter into any Treaty, Alliance, or Confederation, …No State shall,… enter into an Agreement or Compact with another State or with a foreign power…" The counties and cities that are members of ICLEI in the U.S. through its national organization are attempting to implement foreign policy, which our Constitution forbids. What mayors and municipal governments are doing is plain unconstitutional.

"Mayors and local governments set forth the following commitments to implement sub-national, national, and international frameworks by providing resources, authority, and mandate to carry forward climate protection roles and responsibilities."

There is no law or act of Congress to authorize the aiding and abetting of globalism by state and local governments. We have to protect our sovereignty by banning cities and counties to be members of ICLEI, an organization that promotes United Nation's Agenda 21"smart growth" which is detrimental to American economic interests, liberty, and sovereignty.

White House Executive Order on Rural Council

On June 9, 2011, an Executive Order established the White House Rural Council with 25 executive branch departments. It was several days before people paid attention, prompted by my article which broke the story.

"To enhance the Federal Government's efforts to address the needs of rural America, this order establishes a council to better coordinate Federal programs and maximize the impact of Federal investment to promote economic prosperity and quality of life in our rural communities." As a world traveler, I can attest that Americans already have the highest standard of living in rural areas, prosperity, and excellent quality of life when compared to anybody else.

This piece of legislation from the Oval Office established unchecked federal control into rural America in education, food supply, land use, water use, recreation, property, energy, and the lives of 16% of the U.S. population. The order chose the rural population because they "supply our food, fiber, and energy, safeguard our natural resources, and are essential in the development of science and innovation." He who controls the food, land, and water, controls everything else.

Section 1, Policy states, "Sixteen percent of the American population lives in rural counties. Strong, sustainable rural communities are essential to winning the future and ensuring

American competitiveness in the years ahead." What kind of future are we supposed to win? Our rural areas are very successful, they are the number one exporters of corn and wheat to the rest of the world.

There is no definition what rural America is. In fact, there are no definitions in this Executive Order at all. I emphasized the word "sustainable" because it is part of the "sustainable growth" plan of United Nation's Agenda 21. Think of "sustainable" as what is acceptable to the federal government.

Why do we need a rural program? Is this not the ultimate trap to force us into Agenda 21 compliance of One World Government? All rural communities already have education, local laws, state laws, hospitals, and an enviable quality of life.

This order is taking control over our existing executive bodies in the state and local governments. They will do so through federal grants with strings attached, enticing struggling farmers to accepting them as a short-term solution, thus entrapping them into future abdication of property, water, and agricultural land use. The feds are not helping them, they are stepping in to enslave. The government never gives "something for nothing."

The order promises to "expand outdoor recreational activities on public lands." The feds have already curtailed access to water use and public lands in many states through EPA regulations or appropriation of land such as in California and Utah. The fact that they are planning to expand land use for recreation is a joke in itself.

The feds will control local governments through supplemental grants that will be hard to reject in times when revenues are dwindling and budgets are falling short of local needs. Local governments will no longer be able to voice opinions and concerns and citizen grievances will be ignored.

Local governments will no longer be able to set policies without feds approval. Cap and trade implementation will be forced in rural areas and nobody will be able to stop it. Land use, public planning, and food production will be regulated by unelected federal bureaucrats who will set quotas of food production, water use, energy use, and land use. Based on my experience and history, central government planning has terrible consequences, causing shortages, disruptions, famine, and even death.

There will be more federal jobs, more political appointees, no elected representatives, at a time when we are broke, cannot afford, and should not borrow more money from China at the rate of 41 cents for every dollar spent.

Agenda 21 is the program of One World Government to de-grow our economy by controlling every aspect of what we do and how we live. In their view, we deserve to be punished for having polluted the globe through our expansionist economic policies that have kept third world countries backwards. No mention is ever made of the corrupt presidents that rule these third world countries who are responsible for the sorry economic state of their respective dictatorships.

Twenty-five federal agencies are charged with total control of rural life: Department of the Treasury, Department of Defense, Department of Justice, Department of the Interior, Department of Commerce, Department of Labor, Department of Health and Human Services, Department of Housing and Urban Development, Department of Transportation, Department of Energy, Department of Education, Department of Veterans Affairs, Department of Homeland Security, Environmental Protection Agency, Federal Communications Commission, the Office of Management and Budget, the Office of Science and Technology Policy, the Office of National Drug Control Policy, the Council of Economic Advisors, the Domestic Policy Council, the National Economic Council, the Small Business Administration, the Council on Environmental Quality, the White House Office of Public Engagement and Intergovernmental Affairs, and the White House Office of Cabinet Affairs.

Why is the Homeland Security Department involved in rural planning and land use? Should they be when they have no oversight, they can do as they please? They answer to Sen. Joe Lieberman only who then reports to the president.

The Domestic Policy Council and National Economic Council will coordinate this executive order. Why do we need to control 16% of the population that lives in rural areas? Because rural Americans still have control over resources, over our food supply, and they are resistant to globalization. Whoever controls the food supply controls the population.

Once rural areas are controlled by the fed, there will be no resistance, and rural life as we know it, will no longer exist. They will target certain regions, town by town, through ICLEI, until we are compliant with Agenda 21 goals, which are to stop energy development, energy use, and land use. Conservation of all resources to the point of de-growth will have a bearing on population control. Once we are enslaved, there will be no mitigated resistance.

The government will work under false pretenses, using Homeland Security with its unlimited power and resources and other departments, through school districts, grants, agricultural associations, farm banks, police, and other local organizations.

Global government is real, it is here, and we are ignoring the signs, the rules, regulations, appointments, Patriot Act, executive orders, and the newly created councils. We no longer have three branches of government, a two party system, checks and balances, the rule of law, justice, or a Constitution that is followed.

Attack on U.S. Sovereignty - The Law of the Sea Convention (LOST)

Adopted in 1982, The Law of the Sea Treaty was initially called the Third United Nations Convention on the Law of the Sea (UNCLOS III) and aimed to implement a set of detailed rules that would control the oceans, replacing the 1958 (UNCLOS I) and 1960 (UNCLOS II) United Nations Conventions on the Law of the Sea. The European Union and 162 countries have joined the Convention.

"Negotiated in the 1970s, the Law of the Sea treaty was heavily influenced by the New International Economic Order, a set of economic principles first formally advanced at the United Nations Conference on Trade and Development (UNCTAD) in the 1970s and 1980s," calling for redistribution of wealth to the benefit of third world countries.

President Ronald Reagan rejected the treaty in 1982 because it demanded technology and wealth transfer from developed countries to developing nations as well as adopting regulations and laws to control oceanic pollution. Jurisdictional limits on oceans included a 12-mile territorial sea limit and a 200-mile exclusive economic zone limit. The treaty would regulate economic "activity on, over, and beneath the ocean's surface."

In spite of the many pros and cons, in March 2004, the U.S. Senate Foreign Relations Committee recommended by unanimous vote that the U.S. sign the treaty.

Sen. Mike Lee (R-Utah), member of the Committee on Energy and Natural Resources' Subcommittee on Water and Power, opposes the Law of the Sea Treaty (LOST) on several grounds, including the loss of national sovereignty.

In order to ratify a treaty, the President needs two-thirds majority vote from the Senate. According to Sen. Mike Lee, treaties must represent U.S. economic and security interests. Our economy and navigation rights have not been affected by the fact that we chose to reject the treaty. He finds the loss of national sovereignty and mandatory dispute resolution included in the Law of the Sea treaty quite troubling.

The International Seabed Authority ("the Authority") has the power to distribute "international royalties" to developing and landlocked nations. "So hypothetically, a U.S. company that has invested hundreds of millions of dollars in developing clean and safe deep-sea mining machinery would be forced to give a portion of its profits to countries such as Somalia, Sudan, and Cuba – all considered to be developing nations by 'the Authority.'" (Sen. Mike Lee, R-Utah)

Sen. Mark Begich, D-Alaska, chairman of the Subcommittee on Oceans, Atmosphere, Fisheries, and Coast Guard, supports the ratification of the Law of the Sea Treaty (LOST). He believes that this treaty provides rules to handle future underwater minerals, gas, and oil exploration and shipping on new water routes opened by receding Arctic icepack. His support is predicated on the premise that the Arctic icepack melt will be a constant in the future.

Sen. Mark Begich said, "The United States is the world's leading maritime power. Only by ratifying the treaty can it protect freedom of navigation to advance our commercial and national security interests, claim extended continental-shelf areas in the Arctic – an area believed to be twice the size of California – as other nations are already doing, and use its provisions to protect the marine environment, manage fisheries and appoint Americans to help resolve disputes." (The American Legion Magazine)

According to the Heritage Foundation, innocent passage through an area is already protected under "multiple independent treaties, as well as traditional international maritime law." Few countries deny passage to the U.S., given its naval superiority. Under the Law of the Sea Treaty, "intelligence and submarine maneuvers in territorial waters would be restricted and regulated." It is thus not in the national security interest of the United States to ratify this treaty.

The treaty requires policies that regulate deep-sea mining, requires rules and regulations to control and prevent marine pollution, and requires the control of corporations who cannot bring lawsuits independently. They must depend on the country of origin to plead their case in front of the United Nations agency.

"Some proponents of the treaty believe that it will establish a system of property rights for mineral extraction in deep sea beds, making the investment in such ventures more attractive."

President Reagan objected to the Principle of the "Common Heritage of Mankind," which dictates that marine resources belong to all mankind and cannot be exploited by one nation.

To spread the wealth, the UN "Authority" must regulate and exploit mineral resources by asking companies to pay an application fee of half a million dollars, recently changed to $250,000, and to reserve an extra site for the Authority to "utilize its own mining efforts."

A corporation must also pay an annual fee of $1 million and up to 7% of its annual profits and share its mining and navigational technology. Mining permits are granted or withheld by the "Authority" which is composed of mostly developing countries. (Heritage Foundation)

Any kind of maritime dispute, fisheries, environmental protection, navigation, and research, must be resolved under this treaty through mandatory dispute resolution by the UN court or tribunal which limits autonomy. Disputes should be resolved by U.S. courts. (Heritage Foundation)

The United States provisional participation in the Laws of the Sea treaty expired in 1998. Should we consider the ratification of another treaty that has the potential to further chip away at our National sovereignty?

The GOP has recently passed (January 14, 2012) a resolution exposing United Nations Agenda 21 as "a comprehensive plan of extreme environmentalism, social engineering, and global political control that was initiated at the United Nations Conference on Environment and Development (UNCED)."

"According to the United Nations Agenda 21 policy, National sovereignty is deemed a social injustice." United Nations treaties and programs want to force "social justice" through socialist/communist redistribution of wealth from developed nations like the U.S. to third world countries.

The LOST treaty was rejected in 2012 because it did not garner sufficient signatures in the Senate for passage – 2/3 is required. The ratification of the treaty will resurface once the composition of the Senate changes.

Open Government Partnership and United Nations Agenda 21

As Americans are trying to make sense of and understand the multi-faceted United Nations Agenda 21, new information emerges daily. Adopted, signed into law, and implemented through non-governmental organizations "sub-rosa" work since 1992, UN Agenda 21 grows at the local, state, and federal levels with new rules, regulations, executive orders, private-public partnerships, and declarations, accelerating the United States' inclusion into one world government.

Aggressive advertising by compliant progressive media is brainwashing unsuspecting Americans that UN Agenda 21 is protecting the environment and, to oppose it, would mean opposing the preservation of the environment, the destruction of the fragile eco-system, rejection of alternative, green energy, and selfish neglect of their children's future.

The Solar Decathlon 2011 (September 23-October 2) presented by the U.S. Department of Energy, in concert with several universities (Purdue, Middlebury College, Florida International, Ohio State, University of Maryland, University of Tennessee, Rutgers, Massachusetts College of Art and Design, University of Massachusetts, the City College of New York, Hampton University, Old Dominion University, the Southern California Institute of

Architecture, California Institute of Technology, University of Calgary, Team China, Team Belgium, New Zealand's Victoria University of Wellington, and University of Illinois) has displayed at West Potomac Park near Tidal Basin in Washington, D.C. exhibits showcasing how "to create an energy-efficient home, selecting and operating a solar-electric system, and building a more sustainable future." The entire exhibit was tailored for "green building professionals."

During the same month, Solyndra, the California-based solar panel maker filed for bankruptcy protection on September 6 and fired all its 1,100 employees. With much White House fanfare, Solyndra received a $535 million loan guarantee, which was later granted by the Obama Administration. Private investors forked more than $1 billion into the company. It was alleged that investors and executives with Solyndra were substantial donors to Obama's campaign and had spent large sums on lobbying.

Two other companies working on "alternative energy," the darling phrase of liberals, have filed for bankruptcy because they could not compete with China's subsidized solar panels and demand was low. Both companies received money from the $800 billion stimulus.

Solar panels have been subsidized by our federal government and states have given subsidies to taxpayers in the form of tax write-offs for the installation of solar panels. Cliff Stearns (R-Florida) said, "So I think the administration is on this fervent religion of green jobs and clinging to the idea that solar panel is the answer and it is not the answer."

Fox News reported that Evergreen Solar Inc. received "$5.3 million of stimulus cash through a state grant to install 11,000 photovoltaic panels at 11 colleges and universities, a recycling facility, and an education center in Massachusetts."

SpectraWatt from New York, a solar cell company, received a $500,000 grant from the National Renewable Energy Laboratory from the stimulus package to improve solar cells without changing current manufacturing process.

Close to sixteen percent of the labor force is unemployed and cannot afford to pay for the homes they currently own and rent, much less purchase solar panels. Through Agenda 21 requirements, Americans will eventually have to build or retrofit their homes with solar energy in order to meet the United Nations' green agenda. The federal government is mandating the UN Agenda 21 infrastructure of the new "green" alternative energy, solar and wind, while discouraging the use of fossil fuels such as oil, coal, and natural gas.

Under the noble mantra of saving the earth, the United Nations wants to change the way we live, eat, learn, communicate, and move by controlling the economy, the environment, our health, and private property in the name of social equity (social justice). The ultimate goal is to have a one-world government under the aegis of the United Nations, controlled by a handful of individuals.

To bring us ever closer to this goal, world leaders congregated on September 20 at New York City's Waldorf Astoria hotel in advance of the United Nations General Assembly, in order to formally launch a new initiative called the Open Government Partnership. During the day of discussion, they unveiled and signed the "Declaration of Principles."

President Obama called at last year's General Assembly for "specific commitments to promote government transparency." Eight countries have endorsed the Open Government Partnership on September 20, 2011 and are publicly releasing open government plans:

- Brazil
- Indonesia
- Mexico
- Norway
- Philippines
- South Africa
- United Kingdom
- United States

Under **Increase the availability of information about governmental activities**, which sounds benign and helpful to taxpayers, the first sentence is chilling. "Governments collect and hold information on behalf of people, and citizens have a right to seek information about governmental activities."

Under **Support Civic Participation**, one sentence stands out. "We commit to protecting the ability of not-for-profit and civil society organizations to operate in ways consistent with our commitment to freedom of expression, association, and opinion." What happens when citizens' opinions diverge from UN's commitment to freedom of expression? Why do not-for-profit non-governmental organizations (NGOs) need protection if their goals are not nefarious? Why is it fine for liberals to express their opinions as long as the conservative opposition is in complete agreement with them?

Under **Implement the highest standards of professional integrity throughout our administration**, the commitment to have "robust anti-corruption policies" is scary. "We commit to maintaining or establishing a legal framework to make public information on the income and assets of national, high ranking public officials." This brings to mind the economic police we used to have under communism. If a person's income was reported by informants as excessive, the culprits were arrested, fined, and their excess-capacity goods or income confiscated. According to this principle, an informant would be protected. This duality seems redundant since we already have whistleblower laws in place in this country. "We commit to enacting and implementing rules that would protect whistleblowers." There will be "anti-corruption prevention and enforcement bodies." UN seems unable to control their own corruption yet are going after corruption in other countries via an economic and financial police?

Although this signed declaration is non-binding and voluntary, thirty more countries are expected to join. The most astonishing detail is the fact that one of the "featured, leading private sector, non-profit and government innovators in the 21st century" is Socrata, Kenya's Open Government Portal. There is a crass contradiction here in naming Kenya as a leading innovator in anything.

"We commit to espouse these principles in our international engagement, and work to foster a climate of open government that empowers and delivers for citizens, and advances the ideals of open and participatory 21st century government." I thought we elected officials and hired bureaucrats to run our government. When did we turn into a participatory 21st government?

This document is one of many partnerships and initiatives signed by our government's representatives to move us one step closer to a United Nations' led global economy and the erasure of our sovereignty.

UN Agenda 21 and Plan Maryland

On October 31, 2011, Carroll Country Board of Commissioners held a forum in Pikesville to discuss "Plan Maryland." The international panel members included Lord Christopher Monckton, Wendell Cox, Patrick Moffitt, George Frigon, and Ed Braddy.

Lord Christopher Monckton was a science policy advisor to Prime Minister Margaret Thatcher, a contributing author to the Science and Public Policy Institute, and a frequent speaker on climate change science.

An expert in urban planning and transportation policy, Wendell Cox is the principal of an international urban policy firm and senior fellow at the Institut Economique de Montreal in Quebec. A visiting fellow at the Heritage Foundation, Wendell Cox is very concerned about anti-sprawl policies and opposes "densifying" urban areas because it contributes to air pollution levels thus posing health hazards.

Patrick Moffitt served under the Clinton/Gore administration on the White House committee on environmental technology and was president of U.S. Water LLC.

George Frigon is co-chair of the advisory board for the graduate part-time program in Environmental Engineering and Science at Johns Hopkins University and wastewater treatment expert. He is the co-author of the USEPA's manual for wastewater treatment for small communities and senior partner at New Fields, a global environmental consulting firm.

Ed Braddy is the executive director of the American Dream Coalition, which conducts forums on urban planning, transportation, land use, housing and property rights. He opposes smart growth policies.

An environmental group that supports UN Agenda 21 smart growth plans, "1000 Friends of Maryland," called the forum an "absurd event." Apparently freedom of speech is only reserved for liberals. If it exercised by conservatives, it becomes an absurd event.

The panelists were invited by the Carroll County Board of Commissioners to discuss Plan Maryland, a "smart growth" strategy proposed by the state to stop urban sprawl and concentrate development in "approved" urban centers.

"Plan Maryland" is an executive action by Governor O'Malley to preserve 400,000 acres of forest and farmland over the next 20 years. His action does not require legislative approval. Members of the Carroll County commission object to the plan because it shifts control of land use from local elected officials to "unelected state bureaucrats."

The spokesperson for the Maryland Department of Planning, Andrew Ratner, described the expert panel that convened to discuss "Plan Maryland" as "fairly loaded" because, in his opinion, "some of the speakers' areas of expertise have nothing to do with Maryland."

"Plan Maryland" has been controversial in Carroll County because the commissioners have strongly opposed the state's sustainable growth plan, "arguing that it is not about the environment and smart growth but about control and politics." Such politics follow the United Nations Agenda 21 goals of returning millions of acres of land to wilderness by moving populations into approved high-rise, mixed-use, densely populated areas in designated cities around the country.

Senate Minority Whip E. J. Pipkin stated that Governor O'Malley is "at war with rural Maryland." O'Malley is using a 37-year old law to withhold state funding from local governments who refuse to cut urban sprawl. He wants to ban most new septic systems, essentially bringing rural development to a halt.

Additionally, O'Malley had planned an expensive offshore development of wind turbines, higher taxes for transportation, a massive toll increase, a triple sewer "flush tax" by the end of 2011, and gasoline tax increases and the Chesapeake Bay cleanup that will cost counties billions of dollars and many jobs. (Washington Post) Farmers were angry that the Maryland governor was dictating from Annapolis how "communities across the state should develop, and it's wrong, it's arrogant."

As O'Malley's spokesperson, Rachel Guillory, defended his decision, she validated the power grab. "He is basing his decision on what is best for Maryland now and in the future." One wonders how his liberal ideology makes the governor eminently qualified to make such permanent life-altering decisions for the state's citizens without voter and legislative input.

O'Malley's "Plan Maryland," a statewide blue print of land use that mimics UN Agenda 21, is approaching completion. It maintains 400,000 acres as agricultural or forest land and spares it from development that could have happened in the next 20 years. O'Malley's executive order allows development only in "approved" growth areas along the Baltimore-Washington corridor.

If local governments refuse to build more dense housing developments, state funding for school construction and other community projects will be denied as punishment for non-compliance.

O'Malley declared in August 2011 that homes on two-acre plots with septic system were urban sprawl. Homes built within city limits on half-acre plots in range of sewer hookups were not considered sprawl. (Washington Post)

To turn his plan into reality, O'Malley used a 1974 law, without further hearings or action from the General Assembly. He claimed savings of $1.5 billion annually for roads that will not be built to new developments and hundreds of millions needed to expand and improve water and sewer systems.

The panelists in Carroll County, with sound science-based arguments, debunked some of the premises behind "Plan Maryland."

Despite vehement protests, O'Malley enacted "Plan Maryland" without legislative approval. Citizens objected loudly that a state should not dictate by executive order where communities grow.

Protecting property rights and freedoms are guaranteed in the Constitution and should be paramount to the wishes of any individual or environmental group who trample on people's rights under the arrogant excuse that government knows best in their ever-encroaching power and control over our lives.

As Friedrich August von Hayek so aptly expressed it in his Road to Serfdom, the pervasive control "hinders, compromises, enervates, extinguishes, dazes, and finally reduces each nation to being nothing more than a herd of timid and industrious animals of which the government is the shepherd."

No Child Left Inside Act

On June 21, 2011, the Maryland State Board of Education announced that students must be environmentally literate before they can graduate from high school. Each child must receive a comprehensive, multi-disciplinary environmental education aligned with the Maryland State Environmental Literacy Standards.

"This is a momentous day not only for Maryland but for educators across the country who are watching what Maryland does, and hoping to increase outdoor learning in their states," said Don Baugh, Director of the No Child Left Inside Coalition.

Governor O'Malley proudly repeated the Mother Earth stewardship mantra, "Only through exposure to nature and education about our fragile ecosystem can we create the next generation of stewards." Therein lies one of the fallacies of the left, the ecosystem is not really that fragile – the earth has undergone many life-altering disasters and the ecosystem survived and thrived.

The sponsor of the No Child Left Inside Act was Congressman John Sarbanes. "No Child Left Inside will pave the way for a new era of environmental stewardship in this country." The No Child Left Inside Coalition claimed a "national partnership of over 2,000 business, health, youth, faith, recreational, environmental, and educational groups representing over 50 million Americans. The chapter in Maryland boasted over 225 group members, and represented over 635,000 Marylanders." Careful inspection of the list revealed zoos, day camps, recreational parks, and national and international environmental groups.

No Child Left Inside Act was an environmentalist legislative effort encouraged at the national and state levels with a pro green, pro environment, pro global warming, and pro smart growth propaganda as part of k-12 interdisciplinary education.

The sponsors of the bill claimed that "studies show environmental education has a measurable, positive impact on student achievement not only in science but in math, reading, and social studies. Business leaders also increasingly believe an environmentally literate workforce is critical in a burgeoning green economy. Where is this "burgeoning green economy?"

"Field experiences and related activities, when part of the regular school curriculum in environmental education, also help students become healthier." A few biased university College of Education lab experiments made such a claim.

I found plenty of data showing the dismal state of education and schools in Maryland in math, science, and reading. Students can barely read, write, balance a checkbook, or solve simple math problems yet are now required to be stewards of the environment and explore it in depth across the curriculum. Sarbanes believes that a more holistic approach to the curriculum is necessary. Somehow holistic does not mesh well with curriculum. It sounds like a College of Education new age, feel-good teaching method of the moment; let us throw $500 million in this "green" direction. We failed at teaching students to read, write, and compute, perhaps we can be successful in brainwashing them into believing that human activity is bad, causes global warming, and destroys the planet.

Who knew that environmental study and "green play" help children cope with ADD and ease obesity rates? I thought proper nutrition, PE classes, competitive sports, and recess time were designed for physical exercise and thus weight control. What is "green play" anyway?

Maryland politicians and educators claim that environmental study helps with "nature deficit disorder." The term "nature-deficit disorder" was coined by author Richard Louv in his dramatically titled book "Last Child in the Woods" to describe what happens to young people who become disconnected from their natural world. Louv links lack of nature to some of the most disturbing childhood trends, such as the rise in obesity, attention disorders, and depression.

This reminds me of Rachel Carson's book, "Silent Spring," who claimed that DDT killed all the birds, hence the title. Her book started the environmental movement in the U.S. DDT was banned for agricultural use in most developed countries in 1968. Three million people around the globe die unnecessarily each year of mosquito-induced malaria because of Rachel's half-baked book of irrational statements.

The No Child Left Inside Act gives "American students the knowledge that they will need to make informed personal decisions and act as responsible citizens as they face environmental challenges that previous generations never imagined." This is Agenda 21 Armageddon scare tactics to frighten Americans into global compliance to its goals of severely limiting the use of water, electricity, transportation, and denial of human access to wilderness areas all in the name of nature conservation and environmental stewardship.

Americans have been stewards of our environment for generations and resolved issues without any special interdisciplinary curriculum indoctrination from k-12 grades. Maryland curriculum writers are very vague when referring to environmental challenges previous generations never imagined?

The law claims, "environmental education also promotes higher-order thinking skills and is correlated with higher test scores in math and reading." There is no such evidence and no way to prove that higher test scores are actually connected to environmentalism.

The statement, "Environmental Education is the foundation for creating the green workforce of the new economy," is a clear intent of this new curriculum, the brainwashing of our children into the Global Management System (GMS), a world-wide blue print for international totalitarian control of earth and resources, including human resources, under the fuzzy excuses that children are fat, need play time outdoors, and re-connect with nature while their ADD symptoms are "treated." Where is this "green workforce" and where is "the new economy?" Is this another example of non-existent shovel-ready jobs? We have 23 million Americans unemployed and underemployed under the Obama administration and many other millions out of the labor force, discouraged workers who have given up looking for a job.

National coalition members who support the No Child Left Inside Act in Maryland include:

- Adventure Treks

- African American Environmentalist Association
- Alliance for Climate Education
- Alliance for Community Trees
- American Camp Association
- American Canoe Association
- American Cave Conservation Association
- American Deer & Wildlife Alliance
- American Forest Foundation
- American Horticultural Society
- American Recreation Coalition
- American Rivers
- American Sail Training Association
- American Society of Landscape Architects
- American Sports fishing Association
- American Trails
- Biosphere Foundation
- The Early Development of Global Education
- Earth Day Network
- Earth Force, Inc.
- Forest Service Hispanic Employees Association
- Global Green USA
- Global Youth Leadership Institute
- Greening Youth Foundation
- National Hispanic Environmental Council
- National Project for Excellence in Environmental Education
- Sierra Club
- World Forestry Center

There are International supporters of the No Child Left Inside Act in Maryland:
- African Volunteer Football Academy for the Less privileged (AVFAL) (Cameroon)
- Assiniboine Park Conservancy (Canada)
- Patgiri (India)
- Istituto Pangea Onlus (Italy)
- Citizenship Leadership Training Centre (Nigeria)
- Equilibri Naturali

- NOTL Sustainability Network
- NOTL Sustainability Network (**Green Feet People**) is a "non-profit community environmental organization whose mandate is "greening NOTL one step at a time". This includes promoting the sustainability of the housing sector, food systems, energy, water and materials consumption, education, transportation and health." NOTL Sustainability Network is one of the thousands of ICLEI (International Council for Local Environmental Initiatives) local chapters in our cities and counties, which are tasked with "smart growth" to usurp property rights and Constitutional rights. They persuade local officials to revise zoning laws to fit into a "smart code zoning template." As a result, a massive reshuffling of property rights takes place in the name of "greening" the environment.

The No Child Left Inside Act is an insidious spreading of the United Nations Environment Programme (UNEP) which prepared the Global Biodiversity Assessment of the state of the planet in order to validate the Global Management System (GMS) by using doomsday predictions:
- Population reduction
- Oppressive lifestyle regulations
- Coercive return to earth-centered religions
- Self-sustaining human settlements

"Environmental education provides critical tools for a 21st century workforce," says the No Child Left Inside Act. There is, however, a stark distinction between education and indoctrination. These people are engaging in indoctrination, not education. Students already receive ecology and geology lessons incorporated into the curriculum throughout their school life. Taking environmentalism to higher elevations than reading, writing, and arithmetic is plain socialist indoctrination. Advancing UN Agenda 21 as a global contract of the 21st century is wrong. Educators have not received a mandate to change the way we live, eat, earn, learn, work, and survive under the aegis of "Save the Earth."

"The vast majority of Americans are convinced that the environment will become at least one of the dominant issues and challenges of the 21st century, as the growing needs of the growing global population increasingly presses up against the limits of the earth's resources and ecosystems." This is a Malthusian prediction that has population reduction and control written all over it. As Malthus was wrong in his predictions, so are the environmentalists.

Charles O. Holliday, Jr., chairman and CEO of DuPont, declared that "an environmentally sustainable business is just good business, given the growing concern for environmental problems across America. A key component of an environmentally sustainable business is a highly educated work force, particularly involving environmental principles." Inventing the catchy "environmentally sustainable business" term does not reflect the real world possibility of doing business affordably under the dictates of environmentalism. As a matter of fact, many businesses are closing doors and hundreds of thousands of people are losing jobs because of the EPA's strict environmental guidelines. The so-called highly educated workforce needed to fulfill the environmentalists' dream is actually dumber and dumber, lacking basic skills of math, reading, writing, and basic knowledge of traditional business, accounting, history, and American government.

Author of "Walk the Talk - the Business Case for Sustainable Development," Charles O. Holliday, Jr. is a member/leader of the "U.S. Council on Competitiveness." This leftist organization emphasizes government/private sector "collaboration." Its Orwellian website congratulates President Obama for his legislative accomplishments in the manufacturing arena. He must be referring to the thousands of jobs President Obama created in other countries such as Brazil, China, Italy, and Mexico.

It is true that children today spend too many hours a day in front of the computer or television. No parent would object to field trips, outdoor play, or caring for the environment. Nobody wants children to be obese. However, forcing a federal law that would spread across the land, indoctrinating children into environmental stewardship smacks eerily of global Marxism.

Parents have no problem with kids getting out of the classroom, for field trips, to learn about ecology, recycling, preservation, and biology. If the state is forcing, advocating, or brainwashing kids to believe that humans are evil, that we shouldn't drive cars, or live on private property, reproduce, all Agenda 21 propaganda, that is a different matter.

Bumping into Agenda 21 at the National Building Museum

I visited the National Building Museum, a private, non-profit organization. The exhibits occupied about ten percent of the building. The rest of the halls were reserved for lectures and other liberal and fundraising activities. The imposing, three-story atrium, was being readied for a lavish fund-raising gala and was being draped in shades of arresting purple, imitating a huge circus tent, three stories high, in line with the leit-motif, "the cirque."

It did not take long to exhaust the exhibits and the Lego construction room, showcasing a few famous landmarks built to scale from hundreds of thousands of grey and clear Lego pieces.

The gargantuan inner Corinthian columns appeared to support the entire building, yet they seemed anachronistic in comparison to the red-bricked exterior surrounded by a yellow freeze of civil war soldiers.

A simple silver plaque listed annual donors to the private museum, a list of unusual people and organizations: USAID, World Bank, U.S. Department of Energy, Rockefeller Brothers, U.S. Department of Transportation, U.S. Green Building Council, Home Depot, Fannie Mae Foundation, Freddie Mac Foundation, American Planning Association, National Association of Realtors, to name just a few.

I thought Fannie Mae and Freddie Mac had received bailout funds and were asking again for round two of handouts from taxpayers to the tune of billions. They are broke but are charitable to private organizations with our taxpayer dollars.

One of the halls was holding a lecture on "temporary urbanism." Being a very curious person by nature, I became intrigued and joined the audience. I was going to learn about the role of streetscape design in attracting retailers, restaurants, and other small businesses to abandoned or neglected urban properties.

The lecturer introduced us to the D.C. Office of Planning Temporary Urbanism Initiative, which "seeks to transform vacant spaces into vibrant destinations and animated showcases" through unique uses in commercial corridors of pop-up buildings made of "repurposed materials and lighting."

The young man was extolling the virtues of the Center for Bits and Atoms at MIT and their rapid proto-typing of housing and Internet through "Fab Labs" working around the world in countries like Kenya, Ghana, South Africa, India, Costa Rica, Norway, and Afghanistan.

I moved on to the museum bookstore, a place usually unavoidable, but this bookstore I had to see. An entire wall of bookshelves from top to bottom was dedicated to Smart Growth, Green Building, Sustainability, and everything Sustainable Green World propaganda. As I was leafing through various expensive tomes, I was struck by the realization that I could not escape the Green Monster of UN Agenda 21 even in a museum. My plan was to spend an enjoyable afternoon learning more about the history of buildings in Washington, D.C., hoping to escape the heavy traffic, the bleak, daily economic outlook, and political news from the Capitol and here I was bumping heads again with UN Agenda 21.

The main exhibit showed samples of building materials, wall covers, and portraits of various architects and philanthropists who contributed to famous buildings around D.C. and the country.

Most interestingly, I found out that the activist and community organizer, Sammie Abdullah Abbott (1908-1990) had built a multiracial, grassroots organization called the Emergency Committee on the Transportation Crisis (ECTC) to halt the building of freeways in the District of Columbia. The headline in 1969 was "Freeway Cancer Hits D.C." ECTC coordinated similar activism across the country. "Congestion cancer" in northern Virginia from insufficient roads is a more accurate description today. Who knew that community organizers and agitators were so powerful so long ago?

ECTC fought the destruction of black neighborhoods in the path of new roadways. The racist propaganda at the time screamed that the North Central Freeway was "A White Man's Road thru a Black Man's Home!"

In the manner of Acorn, ECTC lobbied public officials, picketed Congress and Mayor Walter Washington's home, held sit-ins, and testified at public hearings to prevent construction of the North Central Freeway. They were so successful that a National Coalition on the Transportation Crisis was formed. In 1976, the battle was resolved when the U.S. Department of Transportation paid for the district's share of the Metro and the planned bridges and freeways were never built.

The three concentric rings of expressways proposed in 1950 by the National Capital Park and Planning Commission were never built thanks to this community activist organization. The Capitol Beltway, the single ring completed and a few unconnected segments survive from the proposed inner loop. Now I know why the D.C. area and suburbs are the most congested in the country and who is responsible for the dearth of roads to handle the heavy traffic.

The community activism, which began with curtailing freeways, is now entering phase two, curtailing building "sprawl" in suburbia and rural areas by concentrating population in high density approved zones in order to "save the planet." It was an interesting and fruitful trip to the museum.

Global Warming Cash Cow in Peril

Hillary Clinton has visited Greenland to experience firsthand "global warming." According to James Taylor, the National Oceanic and Atmospheric Administration (NOAA) satellites have shown minimal if any reduction in polar ice caps since 1979 when their satellites were launched. "Whole Viking villages built in Greenland 1,000 years ago during the Medieval Warm Period, remain buried under hundreds of feet of snow and ice." (James Taylor, "Hillary Needs a New Global Warming Travel Agent," Forbes, June 6, 2012)

Progressive liberals in lock-step consensus are not allowing the global warming cash-cow fraud to die in spite of the fact that thousands of real scientists have debunked the notion that humans, with their mundane activities, can cause the global climate to change. A whole industry of snake oil salesmen was born, waiting in the wings to get rich off the sale of carbon credits and the "green" and "renewable" energy. The renewable part is a fallacy in itself – once energy is spent, it cannot be renewed.

Always at the forefront of progressivism, California lawmakers signed into law Assembly Bill 32 (AB 32) called the California Global Warming Act of 2006, a blue print of the UN Kyoto Accord of 1997. The opposition in California organized a rally in Sacramento on August 15, 2012 to protest California Air Resources Board (CARB) and the planned auction of carbon credits as a commodity on November 14, 2012.

CARB operates outside legislative oversight like the EPA. The cap and trade program will be implemented under the leadership of Mary

Nichols and eleven board members appointed by Governor Jerry Brown. Businesses will pay billions of dollars and pass the cost onto hapless consumers. (http://www.cfactsocal.org/)

On the eve of the United Nations +20 Rio Earth Summit in Brazil, the United Nations Environment Program (UNEP) had issued a 525-page report of "dire warnings" that the Earth's strained environmental systems "are being pushed towards their biophysical limits."

The doomsday picture included but was not limited to the melting of the polar ice caps, deforestation of tropical jungles, loss of desert in Africa, out-of-control use of chemicals, and "emptying out of the world's seas." Rising sea levels, floods, droughts, collapse of fisheries, endangered coral reefs, endangered vertebrate species, doubling of greenhouse emissions, pesticide contamination, and other cataclysmic events were some of the consequences compiled in the last three years by a team of 300 UN commissioned researchers.

The conference on sustainable development in Rio de Janeiro on June 20-22, 2012 discussed four of the success stories (eliminating ozone depleting chemicals, phasing out lead in gasoline, more access to water supplies, research of marine pollutants) of the 1992 Rio Conference on Biological Diversity, while lamenting the lack of success in other areas.

President Vaclav Klaus of the Czech Republic, a skeptic of global warming, told UN Secretary General Ban Ki-Moon that he would not attend the Rio+20 Earth Summit. Klaus' 2007 book ("Blue Planet in Green Shackles – What is Endangered: Climate or Freedom?") named environmentalism as the 21st century's biggest threat to freedom, the market economy, and prosperity." (Jennifer Rigby, The Prague Post)

"We have to say goodbye to unrealistic dreams of new sources of power and stop subsidizing these unprofitable sources by posing a burden on the consumer, either individual or corporate." (President Vaclav Klaus, Energy Gas Storage Summit at Prague Castle, May 24, 2012)

"Change is possible," says UNEP executive director Achim Steiner, "Given what we know, we can move in another direction," away from the age of irresponsibility and towards global action. Is this global action changing fundamentally the way we live in order to accommodate the vision for the planet of a few environmental elites who would give precedence and rights to animals over humans?

If increased access to water is a success story, we must tell that to the people of Tombstone, Arizona, who were denied access to water following a devastating fire in 2011 that destroyed pipelines carrying water to a town of 1,600 residents. The only way residents were allowed to restore their water supply was with primitive tools and wheelbarrows, a herculean task since some sections of the pipes were buried under 12 feet of mud, following monsoon type rains and huge boulder fallout. The endangered Mexican spotted owl was the reason why the EPA was imposing such stringent requirements.

The bankrupted farmers in San Joaquin Valley, California, who lost multi-generational farms when the government cut off their irrigation water, may also ask where is their increased access to water supply that the United Nations so proudly boasts. The government purposefully turned large sections of a previously lush and highly productive farming community into a dust bowl.

The UN Agenda 21, although not ratified by Congress, has been quietly implemented all over the country at the local and state levels through the International Council for Local Environmental Initiatives (ICLEI) sponsored initiatives and visioning grants from various federal government agencies (EPA, Department of Energy, HUD, HHS), and NGOs (non-government organizations) such as the Sierra Club.

In light of the fact that it is a violation of the U.S. Constitution for a local or state government representative to collaborate with international bodies, ICLEI changed its name to Local Governments for Sustainability.

Some local and state governments are beginning to understand the private property grab and are pushing back. The state of Alabama passed Senate Bill (SB 477), "Due Process for Property Rights Act," at the end of May 2012, approved unanimously by both State House and the Senate. The governor signed the bill into law, with total silence from the media. The law protects private property rights and forbids any state or local government agency to participate in UN Agenda 21. The law describes briefly how the UN Agenda 21 plan was devised at the 1992 "Earth Summit" in Rio de Janeiro, Brazil. (thenewamerican.com)

Other local boards and representatives, who understand fully what is at stake and stand to benefit directly from their collaboration with ICLEI and implementation of UN Agenda 21 goals, are forging ahead with their plans in spite of their constituents' protests.

The World Bank published a report outlining how it will push economic development that conserves natural resources and controls pollution. Rachel Kyte, World Bank vice president for sustainable development, said, "We don't have to have global agreements. It would be a whole lot easier if we had them, but we can move forward without them." That is a scary proposition in a democracy.

Ban Ki-Moon, UN General Secretary, discussed the newest wealth re-distribution scheme, "Sustainable Energy for All," pushing to eliminate fossil-fuel subsidies.

The journal Nature published an article "Approaching a state shift in Earth's Biosphere" on June 7, 2012. The lead author, Anthony Barnofsky, and its 21 "consensus" coauthors describe how human activity has brought the globe to a tipping point in which "planetary-scale critical transition" to a different environment will occur and the main culprit is international trade. I used to think that the television docudrama, "Life Without People," was a doomsday ridiculous scenario because it did not explain how people suddenly disappeared and all animals and vegetation survived. Consensus of college professors with an agenda sounds compelling, but it is not science. Blaming international trade for global warming is bizarre.

The paper warned, "humans have radically changed 43 percent of the Earth's surface from its natural state" and have exceeded the 30 percent change that supposedly triggered the "last planetary-scale environmental shift 11,000 years ago when glaciers advanced and then retreated." (Juliet Eilperin, Washington Post, June 7, 2012)

Were humans engaging in international trade 11,000 years ago? Did they have cars, factories, planes, boats, and all the other pollutants blamed for the current "dismal state of the planet?" Are humans that ignorant to believe the environmental nonsense that the planet is dying?

UN is Fleecing US and the EU Carbon Tax

The EU charges a carbon emissions fee, an "extra-terrestrial tax." This is viewed by non-European governments as an attack on sovereignty. China's airlines have refused to comply. "Some non-European airlines may have to choose whether to obey the law of their land or that of Europe." Companies refusing to comply would be fined and denied the right to land in the 27 countries that are members of EU.

The European Court of Justice has already rejected the legal basis of a challenge raised in London by North American airlines. Carriers had until April 30 to calculate their damaging annual emissions and to buy polluting rights for 2012. Delta Airlines was the first to add a surcharge to passenger tickets. Each flight will cost us an additional $32 of a round-trip long-distance ticket. The financial gains are substantial for the bureaucrats since 655 million people flew to Europe last year. The United Nations is pushing for a global deal through its International Civil Aviation Organization (ICAO).

The media did not report on the temperature rise in the U.S. during the time period when no airplanes flew after the 9/11 attack, proving that pollution from airplanes does not increase temperatures, on the contrary, it provides a level of cooling protection. (Lord Monckton)

United Nations no longer lives up to its charter of world peace and is indoctrinating children and the population into the green sustainability hoax. UN wants more than the $516.3 million requested from the United States for its regular budget and more than the $2.182 billion requested for the peacekeeping budget.

According to the OMB, in 2009, U.S. contribution to the UN octopus was $6.347 billion. The United States has provided aid to UN since 1945, currently giving 22 percent of UN's operating budget and 27 percent of its peacekeeping budget. (OMB) Aaron Cantor, USAF (retired) perfectly encapsulated the peacekeeping mission of the United Nations "Ready, Aim, Flee."

The Congressional Research Service revealed that we are giving hundreds of millions of dollars of foreign aid to some of the world's richest countries while borrowing billions from them. More specifically, we gave $1.4 billion to 16 foreign countries that hold at least $10 billion in Treasury securities. China received $27.2 million, India $126.6 million, Brazil $25 million, and Russia $71.5 million. Palestinians receive $400.4 million in economic aid, $100 million to support the Palestinian Authority police training, $61.5 million in emergency humanitarian aid after Israel's "assault on Gaza," an actual retaliation for all the rockets fired randomly from Gaza into Israel.

Fritz Vahrenhold and his geologist colleague, Sebastian Luning, published a book, "Die Kalte Sonne" ("The Cold Sun") in which they claim that important research about climate change was hidden and "cries of an impending catastrophe are misleading." "The world is not facing a climate catastrophe." The authors are dismissing the "CO2 lie" – it is not greenhouse gases that cause problems, it is the sun that determines climate change.

The most relied upon source of information on carbon footprint is the climate report produced by the UN's Intergovernmental Panel for Climate Change (IPCC). The report, produced by civil servants and not researchers, is full of misinformation and doubts. Yet countries around the world are basing their policies, carbon credit taxes, and fundamental changes to their citizens' lives on a bogus report produced by bureaucrats.

Many climate researchers question the quality of computer models used to forecast climate change. "Knowledge of the effect of particle from industry, heating, and auto emissions as well as from oceans, volcanoes and from the soil is very low, according to the IPCC report. These particles serve as seeds for clouds, and some estimates suggest that an increase in the cloud cover by just one percent could offset a doubling of the CO_2 in the air."

Making matters worse, a trading scheme is now part of European Union laws. The EU is trading on emissions that would limit the release of "harmful greenhouse gases." Prices for CO_2 certificates have dropped constantly to about half, around $10.60 per metric ton, in spite of the closure of eight German nuclear power plants in 2011 and the increase in demand for coal power. The CO_2 trading system is not working and is producing nothing but deceptive hot air because politicians decide the amount of CO_2 that industries in the EU may emit way into the future.

Why are CO_2 certificates so cheap? Other than the obvious that people understand it is a fleecing scheme, Germany for one spends billions on renewable energy. "With CO_2 certificates so cheap, generating power from environmentally harmful fuels becomes even more than a good deal - which explains why brown coal consumption increased by nearly 4 percent in 2011, bucking the general trend." Emissions trading is not stopping climate change, but actually speeding it up. (Alexander Jung)

Politicians in America and the current administration are fleecing the American public with EPA regulations and zoning restrictions driven by Agenda 21. Do we want to become subservient to the laws of the European Union and United Nations or follow the supreme law of the land, the U.S. Constitution?

The UN Climate Change Summit in Durban

The UN Climate Change Summit in Durban had outlined the mandate to "respect the rights of Mother Earth" by paying a "climate debt," a slush fund to bankroll the activities of a one-world government. I bet you did not know that Mother Earth had rights.

Lord Christopher Monckton said that the treaty "calls for the west to achieve 50 percent CO_2 emissions reduction within the next eight years, a feat that would completely bankrupt the global economy and spark a new great depression, as well as a more than 100 percent reduction by 2050, which presumably could only be accomplished by killing billions of humans to prevent them from exhaling carbon dioxide."

Lord Monckton wrote, "So, no motor cars, no coal-fired or gas-fired power stations, no aircraft, no trains, back to the Stone Age, but without even the right to light a carbon-emitting fire in your caves."

The treaty called for a two degree Celsius drop in global temperatures, which Monckton said, "would kill hundreds of millions and herald a new ice age." So much reduction in CO_2 concentration would "kill plant life and trees on the planet because they need levels of CO_2 above 210 ppmv (parts per million by volume) to survive."

The plan called to disband military forces as they contribute to climate change. UN will become the world army and police of the globe. An "International Climate Court of Justice" will enforce the treaty. This will require paying a "climate debt" and reparations to third world nations if carbon cuts are not drastic. Developed nations are thus responsible and guilty for the weather patterns and they must be punished.

Lord Monckton also wrote that the money will be collected by UN bureaucrats and distributed according to their judgment. "The UN exists for only one purpose: to get more money. That and that alone, is the reason why it takes such an interest in climate change. The Convention's all-powerful secretariat (one world government) has no plans for democratic elections."

The UN has designed new slush funds to enrich its coffers, a tax on shipping and aviation fuel, a worldwide cap and trade, and a new "Green Climate Fund." According to Venezuela's envoy, Claudia Salerno, the Green Climate Fund is "designed to help poor nations tackle global warming and nudge them towards a new global effort to fight climate change." Salerno's statement is problematic for two reasons. First, global warming has been debunked as a scientific hoax, and secondly, it is arrogant for bureaucrats to claim that humans can manage the climate or fight changes in climate. Over the past century, only two inches in water level rise has been measured, so it is disingenuous to say that many areas would be underwater without such draconian measures undertaken at the helm of the United Nations.

The "legally-binding treaty" is likely to pass this time, said Lord Monckton. The discussion centered on major polluters like China and India. The U.S. wants all polluters to be held to the same legal standard on emission cuts, while China and India do not wish their fast growing economies to be encumbered by strict guidelines.

Lord Monckton was not allowed at the conference initially, he had to "parachute in." He represented the Committee for Constructive Tomorrow, which provides "real solutions to dealing with environmental problems that third world nations are experiencing rather than the Marxist party line of eco-fascists who want to punish the West alone and its developed nations."

According to Lord Monckton, the eco-lunatics sent in goons in certain regions of Uganda, killed off the population and then declared the areas "carbon safe zones." "These people are certifiably insane and are waging a sustained, malevolent attack on the West like termite ants." They are going to send in troops to shut down entire industries for non-compliance with their UN Treaty.

Lord Monckton suggested that people should read for themselves the document at climatedepot.com. More than 1,000 international scientists disagree over "man-made global warming" claims.

United Nations fear mongering "scientists" warn that "time is running out to close the gap between current pledges on cutting greenhouse gases and avoiding a catastrophic rise in average global temperatures." UN released reports claim that "delays on a global agreement to cut greenhouse gas emissions will make it harder to keep the average temperature rise to within 2 Celsius over the next century." This Chicken Little, the Sky is Falling warning is so ridiculous, pretending that the UN has the power to stop the eruption of a volcano, a hurricane, a tsunami, or control nature with its demanding third world dictatorships at the helm.

The treaty is based on deliberately erroneous "scientific data" provided by Al Gore and other environmentalist alarmists who claim, "A warming planet has already intensified droughts and floods, increased crop failures, and sea levels could rise to levels that would submerge several small island nations, who are holding out for more ambitious targets in emission cuts."

The fact that solar flares have intensified, the fact that the data suggest, based on temperature readings in the last century, that we are in a global cooling period, are not variables in this international climate calamity travesty.

The Government Accountability Office (GAO) reported in October 2009 that it is "hard for federal, state, and local officials to predict the impact of climate change, and thus hard to justify the current costs of adaptation efforts for potentially less certain future benefits."

Based on opinion surveys of 176 people, with only 61 percent returning the questionnaire, the following issues were identified in reference to a "federal climate service:"

- Translating climate data such as temperatures and precipitation changes into information that officials would need to make decisions
- The difficulty in justifying the current costs of adaptation with limited information about future benefits.

The October 2009 report on climate change adaptation recommended the "development of a strategic plan to guide the nation's efforts to adapt to a changing climate, including the mechanisms to increase the capacity of federal, state, and local agencies to incorporate information about current and potential climate change impacts into government decision making."

On November 16, 2011, GAO released a document, "Climate Change Adaptation," during the testimony before the Subcommittee on Oceans, Atmosphere, Fisheries, and Coast Guard, the Committee on Commerce, Science, and Transportation, and the U.S. Senate.

Based on global-scale models, and we know how reliably scientific those are, GAO suggested that data from such models must be downscaled to a geographic area relevant to decision makers.

GAO testified that "climate change is a complex, crosscutting issue that poses risks to many existing environmental and economic systems, including agriculture, infrastructure, ecosystems, and human health."

The globe has gone through periods of mild to severe climate changes throughout history. Climate change is not something we suddenly discovered and it was never proven scientifically to be the result of human activity. The Little Ice Age which lasted from 1300-1850 was obviously caused by oceanic air flow disturbance, diminished solar flare activity, and intense volcanic eruptions.

We do have ample evidence that the University of East Anglia had hidden or destroyed data that had proven the global warming hypothesis to be a hoax. Thousands of e-mails were released as evidence that data was tampered with by the academics pushing the Marxist environmental agenda.

"The data does not matter. We are not basing our recommendations on the data. We're basing them on the climate models," said Professor Chris Folland from the Hadley Centre for Climate Prediction and Research. Dr. David Frame, a climate modeler at Oxford University stated, "The models are convenient fictions that provide something very useful."

"No matter if the science of global warming is all phony...climate change provides the greatest opportunity to bring about justice and equality in the world," said Christine Stewart, former Canadian Minister of the Environment.

"We've got to ride this global warming issue. Even if the theory of global warming is wrong, we will be doing the right thing in terms of economic and environmental policy," said Timothy Wirth, President of the United Nations Foundation.

"A 2009 assessment by the United States Global Change Research Program (USGCRP) found that climate-related changes – such as rising temperatures and sea level – will combine with pollution, population growth, urbanization, and other social, economic, and environmental stresses to create larger impacts than from any of these factors alone." Thirteen U.S. federal agencies are subscribers to USGCRP.

"According to the National Academies, USGCRP, and others, greenhouse gases already in the atmosphere will continue altering the climate system into the future, regardless of emissions control efforts. Therefore, *adaptation* – defined as adjustments to natural or human systems in response to *actual* or *expected* climate change – is an important part of the response to climate change."

As with UN Agenda 21, it seems that the fix is on climate change and no amount of dissention from the rest of the population or scientific clarity will dissuade the minority policy makers. One world environmental control by the United Nations through its Secretariat is a bad idea for the developed world, it is a bad idea for the United States, and a bad idea for the sovereignty of many developed nations. It is not just bad policy; it is extortion plain and simple.

Environmentalism Goes Spaceship Earth

A new breed of environmentalist do-gooders has emerged, those who call for man to take charge of "Spaceship Earth." On a full-page spread, the Washington Post declared on January 3, 2011 "More and more environmentalists and scientists talk about the planet as a complex system, one that human beings must aggressively monitor, manage and sometimes reengineer. Kind of like a space ship, "Spaceship Earth." In a leftist disingenuous fashion, the paper generalizes and exaggerates the number of environmentalists and scientists who think this way.

"The new way of thinking green" is a departure from "viewing nature as something that must be protected from human beings – not managed by them." Mark Lynas writes in his book, "The God Species: Saving the Planet in the Age of Humans," "Nature no longer runs the Earth, We do. It is our choice what happens from here."

Who knew or even guessed that humans were so powerful that we could determine the movement of the stars, planets, the sun, the moon, weather, hurricanes, tornadoes, earthquakes, floods, tsunamis, volcanic eruptions, and other natural calamities?

Emma Harris, another environmentalist, advocates for an interventionist and managerial role in the "restoration ecology" movement that manages forests and other natural systems.

The wilderness movement of John Muir in the 19th century and Teddy Roosevelt's in the 20th century "sought to draw boundaries between civilization and nature."

Rachel Carson's book, "Silent Spring," giving "detailed" ecological damage such as singing birds disappearing, managed to ban DDT, the only pesticide that kept mosquitoes under control. Three million people die each year from malaria thanks in part to Rachel Carson's unfounded scaremongering.

Eco-protectors cite ice core drillings in Greenland that show a "chemical signature of the Industrial Revolution." What the author fails to mention is that ice core drillings in the Arctic have shown pollution from Roman times when they did not necessarily have an Industrial Revolution and the planet had less, much less than 7 billion people.

"Influential thinkers" believe that invasive species that have stowed away on planes and boats and migrated from one area of the planet to another should no longer be eradicated but "relocated" in order to stay ahead of climate changes." What a huge undertaking that would be, and who will pay for it? What Pandora's box of unintended consequences will be opened then?

Stewart Brand, "the dean of technological environmentalism," a 1960s hippie who wrote "Whole Earth Catalog" in 1968, promoted in his "*Whole Earth Discipline: An Ecopragmatist Manifesto*" the use of genetically modified organisms and nuclear power, "solar radiation management" through cloud-seeding, and "geo-engineering" to control climate change.

Another expert on "greenology," my invented term for the faux science of environmentalism, Albert Borgmann, a professor of philosophy at the University of Montana, is concerned about overreliance on technology "to fix problems that humans have made." I did take a course in philosophy in my lengthy college career and I know that it had nothing to do with science.

Another expert "greenologist," my term for semi-scientists, said that the March 11, 2011 earthquake in Japan "wasn't supposed to be possible." That is because science was only prepared for an earthquake of 8.4 on Richter scale, not a 9.0, and the generated tsunami waves were 18.7 feet high, far exceeding the planned 13 feet.

Nature could have been controlled and harnessed if science would have been more accurate. Generators were located too low. Japan is an island, which by definition, no matter where you locate something, it is going to be low in some areas or possibly below the sea level.

Activist Bill McKibben published "Eaarth" in 2011 in which he advocated for "a new planet, not so pleasant for human beings, with new values and aspirations." In case you are anxious to know what such planet would look like, it will be "decentralized in political power, energy generation and food production." In his mind, decentralized power would prevent "small problems from exploding into societal catastrophes." "The future should belong, and could belong, to the small and many, not the big and few." (Bill McKibben)

In an Orwellian fashion, Richard B. Alley, Penn State climate scientist and author of "Earth: The Operator's Manual," said, "We are as gods and have to get good at it." I personally only recognize one God and I am a mere blink in His plan.

We have been around this type of tribalism, which resulted in extinction from disease, lack of food, lack of energy sources, proper shelter, clothing, draughts, lack of mobility, invasions of pests, and of neighboring tribes. I do not think humanity would like to revisit such a societal organization. Only in the warped minds of a few "greenologists" would return to the sordid and uncivilized past is a great idea. We are not gods and we need a well-organized society in order to live and thrive. If we unite and work in cooperation, we survive. If we divide into small tribes and communities, we fail miserably.

Gender Comes to Climate Change

I bet you did not know that we had an Ambassador-at-Large for Global Women's Issues. I did not realize that global women existed. I did not know that we had a czarina to represent third world female population's interests in our administration. The post was created by President Obama on April 6, 2009.

Ambassador-at-Large for Global Women's Issues, Melanne Verveer, a member of the Council on Foreign Relations, traveled to Durban, South Africa to the United Nations Framework Convention on Climate Change in order "to highlight the critical and largely untapped potential of women to combat climate change." Who knew that women were so powerful that they could affect climate change!

As I read this brief report, I envisioned billions of dollars washing down the proverbial drain with the blessing of an eager administration to re-distribute our "socially unjust" and "unfairly earned, evil capitalist" wealth.

Ambassador-at-Large Melanne Verveer mentioned studies that have shown that women "are on the frontline of, and suffer disproportionately from, the impacts of climate change." I was hard pressed to find any such studies, my search returned empty.

Ambassador-at-Large Verveer stated that women are a "powerful force for finding solutions to climate change across the board, including areas of agriculture, sustainable forest management, and energy access." Because "a small minority of women farmers have

128

access to land tenure" (Food and Agriculture Organization report and we know how reliable UN reports are), women's potential to combat climate change is limited. I was surprised that the simple act of owning land could combat climate change.

Using a generic statement, "studies have shown," without mentioning any studies, Ambassador-at-Large Verveer stated, "women with right to property are significantly more capable of investing in climate-smart agricultural productivity." I had no idea that such a practice existed in agriculture, "climate-smart productivity." It seems that there is no end to the leftist push to justify UN schemes to milk more funds from the United States in order to enrich the coffers of third world dictatorships.

Food and Agriculture Organization (FAO) defines "climate-smart productivity" as "conservation agriculture, integrated pest management, agroforestry, and sustainable diets." This type of agriculture promoted by FAO "sustainably increases productivity, resilience (adaptation), reduces/removes greenhouse gases (mitigation) while enhancing the achievement of national food security development goals."

Modifying and purposefully trying to destroy experienced and accomplished agricultural methods in the name of saving the planet from man-made greenhouse gas emissions in order to pacify a minority of environmentalists with a socialist agenda of "climate justice" is insane.

Developed nations have such highly successful agriculture yields that less than 2.7 percent of the labor force is dedicated to growing food. Americans have spent for a long time 15 percent of their disposal income to buy food. We do not need to resort to hunter-gatherer status in order to please Mother Gaia. There are huge surpluses for export and we are the main exporter of corn. Donations have been made to third world nations adversely affected by draughts, natural disasters, war, famine, or corrupt centralized planners. Programs have been in place for decades to teach successful agricultural methods to third world nations.

According to Ambassador-at-Large Verveer's report, "women have untapped potential for increasing energy access, which directly relates to climate change." In case you are confused, the report continues, "three billion people globally still rely on traditional cookstoves and open fires to prepare food for their families." Since women are responsible for cooking and collecting fuel, the resulting smoke exposure causes an "estimated two million premature deaths annually, with women and children being most affected." She follows that it "puts women at risk of gender based violence." What does climate change have to do with gender based violence? Would less gender based violence decrease climate change? If we were to cook less and eat raw food, would that alter climate change? I wonder if she factored in natural disasters such as volcanic eruptions, the North Atlantic current, and uncontrolled wildfires.

I am trying to understand this climate change contorted logic. Humans use stoves to cook and that causes climate change; females collect wood to burn in the stoves to prepare food and they contribute to climate change; smoke exposure causes premature deaths but women and children are most affected. I still cannot figure out how it causes gender-based violence; I am still scratching my head.

Ambassador-at-Large Vermeer suggested that we have to "build a global market for clean cookstoves" because they impact the climate through "greenhouse gases and short-lived particles such as black carbon." In her opinion, if women were integrated into the supply chain of clean cookstoves, new economic development opportunities would be created for women. She follows with a quote by Secretary Clinton that "women create a multiplier effect in local communities because they disproportionately spend more of their earned income on food, healthcare, home improvement, and schooling."

Now I am totally lost. The Ambassador-at-Large Verveer introduced more variables to the role of women in combating climate change: food, healthcare, home improvement, and schooling, without really explaining how it all ties in with her flawed hypothesis. Since she referenced two more UN organizations, Feed the Future and the Global Alliance for Clean Cookstoves, it is important to note that the Global Alliance is a "private-public UN initiative to save lives, improve livelihoods, empower women, and combat climate change by creating a thriving global market for clean and efficient household cooking solutions."

The Global Alliance for Clean Cookstoves which was launched on September 21, 2010 in Washington, D.C., has 240 partners and the following founders: German Federal Ministry for Economic Cooperation and Development, Government of Norway, Peru, Morgan Stanley, Shell, Shell Foundation, the Netherlands, U.S. Agency for International Development, U.S. Department of Energy,

U.S. Department of Health and Human Services, National Institutes of Health and Centers for Disease Control and Prevention, U.S. Department of State., Environmental Protection Agency, and the United Nations Foundation.

The United States is in the platinum donor category with $5 million dollars, Department of Energy, EPA, Department of State are in the gold donor category with $1-5 million each, along with socialist European nations such as bankrupt Spain and Ireland, the World Bank, and other UN affiliates.

The Department of Energy is awarding "Clean Biomass Cookstove Technologies" grants of $100,000 and $750,000 at a time when our country is broke, unemployment is at an all time high, taxpayers are unhappy, and the administration is demanding that we reduce our consumption of energy.

The World Health Organization data references that 2 million people die annually from smoke inhalation, more than malaria, TB, and AIDS combined. Apparently the fuel, wood, dung, makeshift charcoal, and agricultural waste, are directly responsible for 2 million deaths, particularly in women and children. These third world dictatorships are incapable of running their countries, feeding, sheltering, and caring for their people properly. It is mind boggling and highly suspicious that they can keep such accurate disease and death rate data.

I am not disputing the fact that people have died throughout history from unsanitary and unhealthy living conditions. We have waged education wars to improve living conditions and spent trillions of dollars to alleviate poverty around the world yet we do not seem to be any closer today than we were in the beginning. The corrupt third world governments have stolen the money and personally enriched themselves instead of improving their citizens' living conditions. To continue this pattern is absolute madness.

Ambassador-at-Large Verveer praised the "efforts to build on the gender equality and women empowerment language in the Cancun agreements." It seems that lip service is quite an accomplishment as long as the "language on gender balance related to the composition of the board of the new Green Climate Fund, the Standing Committee, and the Adaptation Committee" are in line with the UN Agenda.

She concluded her report with a reference to the Green Belt Movement, a United Nations organization dedicated to "planting trees, protect watersheds and empower communities across Kenya in 2012." The environmentalist agenda is pushing indigenous forests and *climate justice* for Africa. "The future of not only women but our planet depends on it."

I am disappointed that hard-earned taxpayer dollars go to socialist causes that plan to "fundamentally change" the way we live in the name of environmental justice. How much more waste of American dollars is going to take before taxpayers have had enough? Is it not time for United Nations to move their headquarters to Africa? United Nations is primarily concerned with Africa, controlled by third world dictators, and is not promoting the interests of the developed world at all.

Cook Stoves and Climate Change

The Department of Energy awarded "Clean Biomass Cookstove Technologies" grants of $100,000 and $750,000. According to Washington Post, the U.S. had pledged $105 million in 2011-2012 toward the project and Hollywood provided a famous spokesperson, Julia Roberts. Replacing cook stoves with "clean cook stoves" with chimneys was intended to help 100 million households in third world countries by 2020.

Results from two studies published demonstrated that "clean cook stoves" did not improve the users' health, did not reduce pollution in the environment, did not reduce the amount of wood burned, and "occasionally released a larger volume of certain pollutants than the traditional stoves they were intended to replace." Brian Palmer said in the Washington Post, "From a wider environmental perspective, clean cook stoves didn't slow deforestation and greenhouse gas emissions either."

RESPIRE (Randomized Exposure Study of Pollution Indoors and Respiratory Effects), a large-scale study, showed improved air quality and health but not by as much as suggested in observational studies. (Washington Post)

Rema Hanna of Harvard University and Esther Duflo and Michael Greenstone of MIT released the results of a much larger study, "Up in Smoke." They sold "clean cook stoves" to 2,600 households in 44 Indian villages for 75 cents each. The actual cost of the stoves was $12.50. Made of mud with two burners and a chimney, the stoves were not always used correctly, or maintained by the users. The "clean cook stoves" delivered the same amount of measured pollution as the previous stoves even though people were trained how to use them properly.

"Lung functioning, incidence of respiratory illnesses, the body mass index of children in the household and infant health outcomes such as birth weight and infant mortality did not change significantly." (Brian Palmer, Washington Post, April 17, 2012)

Brian Palmer admitted in his Washington Post column that, "Just because a solution works in a laboratory – or among a small group of closely watched test subjects – doesn't mean it should be rolled out to 100 million households."

Michael Greenstone of MIT said, "This isn't an argument against spending money; it's an argument against spending money unwisely." Yet The Global Alliance for Clean Cookstoves is forging ahead with studies in Ghana, Nepal, and Kenya in spite of failures so far.

I am not disputing the fact that people have died throughout history from unsanitary and unhealthy living conditions. We have waged education wars to improve living conditions and spent trillions of dollars to alleviate poverty around the world yet we do not seem to be any closer today than we were in the beginning. Repeating the same mistakes and expecting a different outcome is a pattern of absolute liberal madness.

Smart Meters and your Health

Following the intense propaganda work of UN Agenda 21, the International Council for Local Environmental Initiatives (ICLEI), non-government organizations (NGOs), and their local affiliates around the globe, including 600 in the U.S., Smart Meters have been installed in many countries. Although U.S. installation has been slower, many European nations are already compliant, as I have witnessed on a recent trip. Even the most dilapidated tenements have shiny Smart Meters installed with EU funds.

Dominion Power in northern Virginia has completed a "pilot" installation in 100,000 homes in three counties. Additionally, the utility is offering $40 "cooling rewards" to each home willing to accept the installation of an A/C cycling switch on a home's cooling system. During "periods of high electrical use, between June 1 and September 30, Dominion may cycle your home's cooling system on and off at defined intervals" during week days. The program is meant to help the utility "manage higher electrical use in the summer and reduces the need to run peak generation or import electricity into our electrical system."

The payoff for helping reduce the "carbon footprint" is the increased customer rates that punish those who are meager in their consumption. Besides the $40 bribe, customers will have the satisfaction of suffering the effects of hot and humid summers in their own homes and knowing that the ruling elite will keep their homes and offices as cool as possible while laughing at the hapless consumers who foot the higher bills for those who make the rules.

Maryland, a progressive state that has been a communist pioneer of UN Agenda 21, has been sweltering in the summer six hours a day during peak consumption and freezing in winter, having installed Smart Meters voluntarily, with financial incentives of $100 and the promise that household electricity consumption will diminish, the carbon footprint will be reduced, and the overall outcome will save the planet from doom and gloom. And I thought Al Gore's carbon credits scheme of global warming had been debunked as a giant manufactured fraud.

Higher than normal utility bills and overbilling from smart meters have lead to lawsuits, including two class-action lawsuits in Bakersfield, California, and Texas. Michael Kelly is a lawyer handling a class-action suit against the state of California's dominant utility, Pacific Gas and Electric over billing disputes.

Smart meters were installed by major investor-owned utilities throughout California. Installation costs were partially paid by customers through additional fees and taxpayers. PG&E has installed about 8 million smart meters in California.

The backlash against smart meters started in 2009 with Kelly's class-action lawsuit claiming rate-payers in Bakersfield were overcharged with bills up to 300% higher than normal.

A study by the Ponemon Institute of 25,000 U.S. adults found that people worried about the impact these meters had on their privacy. The primary concern among those surveyed was the use of personal information by the government.

Many customers had no clue they had a smart meter because most were installed without homeowners' permission or in spite of their protests. The medical impact these radiation-emitting devices on health was not disclosed by the power companies.

The EMF Safety Network collected data on the harmful health impact associated with electromagnetic fields (EMF) and radio frequency radiation (RF). Customers complained of various symptoms within hours of the installation of Smart Meters in their homes:

- Severe and persistent headaches
- Nausea
- Insomnia

- Agitation and irritability
- Difficulty in concentrating
- High pitch ringing in ears
- Depression
- Lethargy
- Forgetfulness
- Heart palpitations
- Buzzing and humming sounds
- Constant fatigue

Oncor Energy Delivery Company of Texas testified before the Public Utilities Company of Texas that a smart meter collector transmits over an area of 125 square miles, approximately 80,000 acres. The signal strength to cover such a large area is considerably higher than previously advertised, prompting a serious public health concern. "The area of transmittal between wireless tower antennas and smart meter routers varies substantially based on geography and customer density. On average, the area for routers on Oncor's system is approximately 5 square miles, and on average, the area for collectors on Oncor's system is approximately 125 square miles." (August 20, 2012)

Original documentation can be found on page 9 at the following link:

http://takebackyourpower.net/wp-content/uploads/2012/09/Responses-to-Questions-from-Public-and-Honeycutt-08-20-12-FINAL.pdf

Captain Jerry Flynn of the Royal Canadian Navy is retired from the Communication Electronics Engineering Branch with expertise on radio frequency, antennas, wireless radio communications, solar storms, solar flares, electromagnetic frequency spectrum, and electromagnetic radiation. He stated, "No informed person can question that microwave weapons exist or that the long term, low intensity EMR emitted by pulsed microwave devices are injurious to not just humans but to all life forms."

The Soviets have experimented with lethal microwave weapons in the 2.4 Hz range, the exact same frequency that Wi-Fi routers, DECT phones, and Zig Bee radios use inside every Smart Meter. (http://takebackyourpower.net/former-canadian-navy-captain-engineer-are-smart-meters-microwave-weapons/)

Customers were not asked for permission to install Smart Metering devices and were told that they cannot opt-out or pay from their own pockets to re-install analog devices. Some citizens were forced to move to other areas or live in their cars. Upon return to an area without smart meters, the symptoms of illness disappeared.

No testing was done on smart meters to back up the claims by government and manufacturers that the meters are safe. The World Health Organization and independent testing revealed that smart meter radiation is a Class 2B carcinogen. (http://stopsmartmeters.org)

According to George W. Arnold, the national coordinator for smart-grid interoperability at the National Institute of Standards and Technology (NIST), "there is no federal security mandate for smart meters." The NIST, an agency of the U.S. Department of Commerce, is not involved in regulations; it is only tasked with promoting standards among industries.

While the Energy Policy Act of 2005 and Energy Independence and Security Act of 2007 were codified into public laws, "No part of them creates a federal law pertaining to individual consumers or dictating that the public must be forced to comply with provisions of Smart Grid." (Marti Oakley)

When I sent a letter to my power company to opt-out, I received a form letter telling me that they have no plans at the moment to install smart meters in our area, however they are safe, and I should visit their website and read their propaganda.

Contrary to manufacturers and utility heads who maintain that there is no "opt out," the consumer must be offered the meter, or request the meter and "opt in." "No one can be forced to comply with an unrevealed contract between private corporations, to which you were never a party and had no knowledge of." (Marti Oakley)

The Department of Energy offered in October 2009 $3.4 billion in stimulus grants to states under the American Recovery and Reinvestment Act (ARRA). The state recipients announced 100 smart grid projects with the rollout of 18 million Smart Meters, 1 million in home energy management displays, and 170,000 smart thermostats, advanced transformers, and load management devices. The award selection was divided into categories:

- Advanced Metering Infrastructure
- Customer Systems
- Electric Distribution Systems

- Electric Transmission Systems
- Equipment Manufacturing
- Integrated and Crosscutting Systems

The Department of Energy $3.4 billion award was the largest amount of ARRA made in a single day. The smart-grid projects competing for $800 million in federal grants under the stimulus program had to meet strict cyber security guidelines, standards, and recommendation for state utility boards and the Federal Energy Regulatory Commission. The two figures did not include the frequent "grant" programs devised to federally subsidize private corporations identified as "stakeholders," with taxpayer dollars.

Cementing a police state while pandering to corporations, Congress flooded the Department of Energy and the Commerce Department with billions of dollars through the Economic Stabilization Act of 2008 and the 2009 Stimulus package in order to buy access to various states.

A meeting with the Council of Governors followed to determine how to flood the states with cash during severe economic problems caused by the administration's mismanagement of the economy, and how to gain control within the boundaries of states. Most governors accepted the free cash influx. A few initially rejected it. The DOE and some unlawfully created "corporate federal agencies" dispersed cash to "stakeholders," various private utility companies.

The American public was forced to subsidize capital investment and expansion of privately owned utilities, in addition to the initial stimulus package coming from taxpayers.

The Energy Policy Act of 2005 http://doi.net/iepa/EnergyPolicyActof2005.pdf) and the Energy Independence and Security Act of 2007 (http://energy.senate.gov/public/_files/RL342941.pdf) passed Smart Meters pertaining to federal buildings and federal housing only, pursuant to the Constitution which gives the federal government power over "needful buildings, insular possessions, and territories." The word "voluntary" preceded any other item.

The "Go Green" constant propaganda, aggressive advertising, policies, huge stimuli, and grants are some of the many reasons why the national debt is out of control. The EPA and its myriad of "green" initiatives are killing jobs in every sector of the economy.

"Going green" is promoted as improving public health and reducing the carbon footprint although most of our electricity is still produced by burning coal and fossil fuels.

The EPA spent $7,180,485,184 on "conservation" programs, mostly aimed at controlling water usage. The "green jobs" created were temporary shows of political pandering. They disappeared quickly after the one-time grant expired and the community had to struggle to find the money to keep the program, leaving more deficits and regulations that further destroyed the economy of the community.

"According to a report by the National Center for Public Policy Research, as a result of new EPA regulations, several utility companies, American Electric Power, Duke Energy, and Southern Company announced they were closing coal-fired plants because of excessive costs to meet the energy's new standards." (Tom DeWeese, American Policy Center)

To enforce UN Agenda 21 Sustainable Development, the state-mandated Comprehensive Development Plans (CDP) is the weapon of choice. The CDP receives its funding from the Energy Efficiency and Conservation Block Grant Program that provides money to communities that participate in the program. To get the federal money, communities have to set regulations for energy efficiency and water conservation. The grant money has been used for mandatory energy audits of private property such as $20,000 in Washington Country, Virginia.

To further control energy and water use, Chesterfield County, Virginia received $2.7 million to reimburse residents who purchased energy-efficient appliances such as washers and dryers. (Tom DeWeese)

The Smart Grid accelerates energy costs; it does not deliver more efficient use of energy. It is a tool of UN Agenda 21 population control and energy control, enabling the energy provider to charge the highest rate possible. It is also a business plan for citizen surveillance without a warrant, extorting the public for corporate profits.

The added bonus for United Nations, who contends that we are overpopulating the earth and thus destroying it, is the people who are getting sick and will eventually die from these meters blasting unsuspecting customers 24/7 with radio frequency radiation that relays information 6-8 times per minute to the utility company. (Marti Oakley)

The EPA blocked the Keystone XL pipeline that would have brought oil from Canadian oil sands to Texas refineries. The construction of the 2,000-mile pipeline could have produced billions of dollars in tax revenue from thousands of construction jobs and the 900,000 barrels a day would have increased our national security and lessened our dependence on foreign oil. This oil and the coal-fired plants that produce electricity could have prevented the smart meter fraud.

Links: World Health Organization (pdf)
http://stopsmartmeters.org/)
http://www.w4ar.com/Smart_Meter_refusal_Letter.pdf
http://stopsmartmeters.org/
http://www.llsdc.org/attachments/wysiwyg/544/usc-pos-law-titles.pdf
http://www.ferc.gov/legal/fed-sta/ene-pol-act.asp
http://www.ferc.gov/industries/electric/indus-act/smart-grid.asphttp://www.ferc.gov/industries/electric/indus-act/smart-grid/eisa.pdf
http://www.seiec.com/Purpa%20II%20integrated%20resource%20planning.html
http://www.jct.gov/publications.html?func=startdown&id=1352
http://jct.gov/publications.html?func=startdown&id=1353
http://www.house.gov/apps/list/press/financialsvcs_dem/press092808.shtml
http://www.kema.com/services/consulting/utility-future/smart-grid/follow-the-money-stimulus-funding-begins-to-flow-into-smart-grid-section.aspx
http://www.govenergy.com/2009/pdfs/presentations/Energy101-Session05/Energy101-Session05-Chvala_William.pdf
http://www.house.gov/apps/list/press/financialsvcs_dem/press092808.shtml
http://www.scribd.com/doc/43043654/US-Smart-Meters-Regulations-Policy-Makers-Guide
http://www.nist.gov/smartgrid/
http://www.scribd.com/doc/43043654/US-Smart-Meters-Regulations-Policy-Makers-Guide

Smart Meter Battles in Nevada

On December 6, 2011, Channel 13, an ABC affiliate, reported that Nevada Energy's Smart Meters were "slammed by customers." The Public Utilities Commission (PUC) approved the $300 million dollar smart meter program in July 2010. After the installation of 600,000 smart meters and thousands of complaints, the PUC decided to give customers the chance for input.

Nevada Energy claimed that smart meters would save them $35 million in operating costs per year. Customers countered that their cost in health and higher bills will be too high. Some were angry because there was no opt-out choice. Other customers claimed that the utility company did not inform them of the existence of a list of postponement. Smart meters were installed without customer consent and notices were sent out after installation.

Customers disagreed with the utilities claim that smart meters were "safer than cell phones and radio frequencies emitted by Earth." Sheila Z. Sterling said, "I think a lot of the science that they're talking about has been skewed."

Customers believed that data collected every 15 minutes would be sold or shared with other entities. Data could be captured by hackers standing outside homes and then sold to the highest bidder.

Many disputed the Nevada Energy claim of 90 percent customer satisfaction. Katrin Ivanoff said, "You answer yes or no to questions and all of a sudden they think you're happy with the installation. Those are two completely different things."

The AARP Director of Government Relations was particularly concerned by "dynamic pricing," when customers cut their own costs by cutting back on power. He believed this feature would not remain voluntary and it was not practical, particular in hot summers for seniors and small children, when turning off air conditioning was not an option.

News 3, an NBC affiliate, reported that the Public Utilities Commission had misled the public by hiding the postponement list and telling customers that they cannot opt-out. Many disbelieving customers were told that smart meters track their energy use and report consumption more accurately than traditional meters.

A doctor testified on behalf of PUC in reference to customers' health complaints about electro-magnetic radiation and radio frequency exposure. The doctor dismissed their complaints as unlikely to be caused by smart meters.

According to Channel 5 Fox News affiliate, some customers' bills went up tenfold, while others went from $100 to $350 per month. Invasion of privacy and hackers were other concerns expressed by Nevadans.

Nevada Energy said their devices were safe. "The exposure in front of the panel outside the house is about one fifteen thousands of the FCC exposure limit." The company insisted that radio frequency (RF) fields from the meters were about "5,000 times less hazardous than signals from the average cell phone." "Frequencies are well below visible UV or other high energy electromagnetic fields." "A lot of these are industry related reports that say that smart meters are o.k., well of course because they're trying to sell us a product," said Joyce Hazard. Besides, cell phones are optional, nobody is forcing consumers to buy cell phones.

Customers wanted to be able to opt out of the program. "Several states on the East Coast have either implemented opt outs or they're considering opt outs, and I hope our commission will consider an opt out also," said Mike Hazard.

The issues were not just privacy, accuracy, cost, security, and health. As Col. Robert Frank (USAF Ret.) indicated, the real issue was the "overall safety and integrity of the national electrical grid." The possibility of a cyber attack and subsequent meltdown of the entire electrical grid from a terrorist hacker was a real possibility. It has happened at the water plant in Illinois in November 2011.

Michael Hazard reported that a workshop was held in response to pressure from a PUCN staff member in Carson City. Nevada Energy admitted publicly that there is no federal mandate for smart meters. However, they will continue to demand smart meter installation of all customers by the end of 2012.

In the meantime, Mr. Hazard suggested that customers, who do not wish to have smart meters installed in their absence, should tape the following signed and dated message to their traditional electric meters. "Attention Utility Company: We refuse to allow you to install a smart meter on our premises. We object to this because of privacy and health issues."

Americans are not giving up easily. On October 4, 2012 a National Day of Action to Stop Smart Meters took place. Take Back Your Power.com has published a form letter on September 25, 2012 drafted by Connie Fogal of the Canadian Action Party which is based on Canadian law to inform utilities companies that customers do not wish to have Smart Meters installed on their properties in British Columbia without their consent. This form letter can be amended to conform to U.S. laws. (http://takebackyourpower.net/new-no-smart-meter-letter-notice-from-connie-fogal/)

The Smart Grid with its millions of smart meters accelerates energy costs; it does not deliver more efficient use of energy. It is a tool of UN Agenda 21 population control and energy control, enabling the energy provider to charge the highest rate possible and to shut down power during higher consumption periods. It is also a business plan for citizen surveillance without a warrant, extorting the public for corporate profits.

Smart Meter Removal

California's Investor Owned Utilities (IOUs) has quietly begun replacing smart meters with analog meters for citizens reporting adverse health effects. Consumer rights and other groups demanded immediately that their wireless devices be removed from their homes.

Joshua Hart of stopsmartmeters.org reported the good news just as PG&E deployed the last phase of its smart meters in California. In California, the utility costs have skyrocketed in spite of the Department of Energy's promise that the smart meters will lower electricity costs.

California's counties and cities have demanded a stop to smart meter installation and some local governments passed laws prohibiting wireless meters. Nevada's Pacific Utilities Company (PUC) called for investigation into the adverse health effects and other smart meter issues.

The California Public Utilities Commission President Michael Peevey assured customers that the utility "will provide for you to go back to the analog meter if that's your choice." The problem is that most Americans have no idea how damaging these smart meters are and an even larger group of Americans have never heard of smart meters. Some see them as a significant contribution to "save" the planet because that is how these meters were sold to the public.

The tired rhetoric promoted the idea that the smart grid and smart meters save the planet from doom and gloom, reduce waste by cutting your electricity at peak usage, eliminates the reader who must go to each home to calculate monthly consumption, reduce carbon footprint, and make the planet "green." The reality is very far from the disingenuous promises.

Californians' electric bills have almost tripled and lawsuits ensued. An analog meter user who insisted on keeping it has to pay $35 each month to have his meter read by the power company. Thousands of customers across the country are having severe to adverse health effects from radiation exposure.

Millions take issue with the power company selling wireless data collected from their homes via smart meters to third parties. The utility company knows if you are home, if you are away, if you are on vacation, which lights are turned on, which appliances, which computers, TVs, and other devices in your home.

Caitlin Phillips of Santa Cruz, Ca, who had suffered severe headaches and other symptoms from her smart meter, became the first person for whom PG&E re-installed on October 28, 2011 the classic analog meter. Caitlin Phillips had told the Wellington Energy installer, a subcontractor of PG&E, that she did not want a smart meter. "When I returned home later, I discovered a smart meter on my house. That night I awoke to severe anxiety, headache, and buzzing in my teeth, and realized the new smart meter was on the other side of the wall from my bed."

Caitlin received help from "Stop Smart Meters" group who referred her to sources to obtain an analog meter and a person to install it. Her symptoms disappeared immediately after the analog meter was installed.

Caitlin spoke to a commission meeting in San Francisco about her ordeal and a week later PG&E crews replaced her temporary analog meter with an official PG&E analog meter. Her frustration, pain, and suffering were finally over.

An "opt-out" proceeding was overseen by an Administrative Law Judge at the California Public Utilities Commission. "There are hundreds of thousands, if not millions, of people suffering in their homes from forced 'smart' meter radiation," said Joshua Hart, Director of the grassroots organization Stop Smart Meters.

PG&E and other utilities have responded to health complaints by replacing wireless 'smart' meters with digital meters that are "wireless-ready." These digital meters have been associated with health problems as well from "dirty electricity" frequencies that pass into a home via the electrical wiring. Digital meters have been rejected by customers who still report health issues after installation. (Joshua Hart)

Susan Brinchman, Director of the San Diego based Center for Electrosmog Prevention, said, "At this point, the burden of responsibility is on the utilities to demonstrate that any new meter they want to install on our homes is safe. Communities have the right to retain analog meters at no extra charge."

While California is pushing back against the wireless technology, places like northern Virginia are going full steam ahead with the installation. "The utilities must respond promptly to all requests that analogs be returned. The alternative is that people will increasingly turn to independent professionals to remove unwanted 'smart' meters from their homes, a reasonable action we assert is within our legal rights. Protecting your family's health is not tampering."

Links:

http://stopsmartmeters.org/

http://www.lasvegassun.com/news/2011/oct/25/nv-energys-smart-meters-be-investigated/

http://sanfrancisco.cbslocal.com/2010/12/29/2-arrests-at-pge-smartmeter-protest-in-marin-county/

http://www.youtube.com/watch?v=4IjC4BEZxLg (Video of the smart meter switch)

Smart Meters Big Brother of Our Day

The American Academy of Environmental Medicine advised on January 12, 2012 in a letter addressed to the Public Utilities Commission of the State of California that they opposed "the installation of wireless smart meters in homes and schools based on a scientific assessment of the current medical literature. Chronic exposure to wireless radiofrequency radiation is a preventable environmental hazard that is sufficiently well documented to warrant immediate preventative public health action." (http://emfsafetynetwork.org/wp-content/uploads/2009/11/AAEM-Resolution.pdf)

"Exposure to levels of radio frequency RF (3KHz-300GHz) and extremely low frequency ELF (300Hz) produced by smart meters warrants immediate and complete moratorium on their use and deployment until further study."

The FCC guidelines that deem smart meters safe are obsolete because they study only "thermal tissue damage and overlook genetic and cellular effects, hormonal effects, male fertility, blood/brain barrier damage, and increased risk of certain types of cancer from RF and ELF levels similar to those emitted by smart meters."

As each home becomes a "wireless telecommunications facility," children are particularly at risk for altered brain development, impaired learning, and behavior.

Current safety limits on pulsed RF are considered "not protective of public health" by the Radiofrequency Interagency

Working Group (FDA, OSHA, EPA, FCC). Emissions of smart meters have been classified by the World Health Organization International Agency for Research on Cancer (IARC) as a possible human carcinogen.

The Congressional Research Service and its legislative attorneys prepare reports for Congress on various issues. Two such reports were issued on smart meters. "Smart Meter Data: Privacy and Cybersecurity" was published on February 3, 2012 and "The Smart Grid and Cybersecurity – Regulatory Policy and Issues" was published on June 15, 2011.

The writers agreed, "unforeseen consequences under federal law may result from the installation of smart meters and the communications technologies that accompany them." In addition, the information "generated from smart meters is a new frontier for police investigations."

The Fourth Amendment requires police to have probable cause to search areas in which people have a reasonable expectation of privacy. Courts deny protection to information a customer gives to a business as part of their commercial relationship. Thus, police can access bank records, phone, and traditional utility records through the "third party doctrine." Technology can erode an individual's privacy even more.

The American Recovery and Reinvestment Act of 2009 gave stimulus money to electric utilities to accelerate the deployment of smart meters to millions of homes via the Department of Energy's Smart Grid Investment Grant Program. Developers thought that the old patchwork infrastructure did not interface, was an arcane system of electricity delivery, and had to be replaced by a nationwide system called the Smart Grid that could be easily controlled and manipulated from a central location.

Smart meter technology is part of the Advanced Metering Infrastructure (AMI). It records near-real time data on electricity usage, it transmits data to the Smart Grid, and it "receives communication from Smart Grid such as real-time energy prices, or remote commands that can alter a consumer's electricity usage to facilitate demand response."

In case you misunderstand what demand response is, here is the official definition. "Demand response is the reduction of the consumption of electric energy by customers in response to an increase in the price of electricity or heavy burdens on the system."

Notice that the reduction in consumption is not defined as voluntary when there is a heavy burden on the system, and it incorporates the promise by the President that our electricity prices will skyrocket.

Smart meters are designed to decrease peak demand for electricity by turning off electricity to customers by remote. Remotely controlled thermostats will also turn off air conditioning units.

HVAC contractors are required to install programmable thermostats on all systems in areas where city officials have inspection authority created by city councils. Thermostats can be overridden by the smart meter so that a home's temperature can also be remotely controlled. RFID tracking tags will be gradually installed in all items purchased, including digital thermostats. Non-digital thermostats cannot be tracked and will thus be banned.

The Department of Energy used the $4.5 billion stimulus to reimburse up to 50 percent of smart grid investments, including the cost to electric utilities of buying and installing smart meters. As of September 2011, the Federal Energy Regulatory Commission (FERC) funded 7.2 million smart meters and partially 15.5 million. The Institute for Electric Efficiency (IEE) expects 65 million smart meters in operation by 2015.

The issues for those who generate, seek, or use the data recorded by smart meters are varied:
- Privacy of electronic communications
- Data storage
- Computer misuse
- Foreign surveillance
- Consumer protection
- Cybersecurity
- Hacking
- Health issues
- Higher energy costs for consumers
- Solar flares
- Electromagnetic pulse (EMP)

The myriad of legal entanglements cannot be predicted. According to Richard J. Campbell, Specialist in Energy Policy, "It is unclear how Fourth Amendment protection from unreasonable search and seizures would apply to smart meter data, due to the lack of cases on this issue."

Smart meter technology measures usage as frequently as once every minute, which appliances a consumer is using, what time of day, if a residence is occupied, how many people reside there, if it's occupied by more people than usual, daily schedules, including times when they are or away from home or asleep, if homes have alarm systems, if they own expensive electronic equipment such as plasma TVs, if they use certain types of medical equipment." (Department of Energy)

Utility providers match data on electricity usage with "known appliance load signatures" and daily schedules by observing when residents use most electricity. U.S. v. Kyllo subpoenaed electricity spreadsheet records because they suspected an indoor marijuana growing operation. Imagine how much easier it would be today with smart meters.

According to Jeffrey Carr, "Health insurance companies could determine if a house uses certain medical devices and appliance manufacturers could establish if a warranty has been violated."

Smart meters collect and store data on names, service address, billing information, networked appliances, meter IP address, transactional records, and identity of the transmitter. Data is sent to the grid via twisted–copper phone lines, cable lines, fiber optic cable, cellular, satellite, microwave, WiMAX, power line carrier, and broadband over power line. Wireless costs less but cybersecurity becomes a huge issue because data is stored within the grid and within the physical world.

Smart meters can give police access to eating, sleeping, showering habits, appliance use and when, TV use, and exercise equipment use. Does this uphold the Fourth Amendment that the "right of the people to be secure in their persons, houses, papers, and effects, against unreasonable searches and seizures, shall not be violated?"

Liberties in the Constitution apply only to actions by the state and federal governments. Utilities can be privately owned, publicly owned, federally operated, and non-profit cooperatives. Under "public records theory, law enforcement can request smart meter data since public records are not afforded Fourth Amendment protection. Law enforcement access to state public records is unrestricted." (Slobogin, Nilson v. Layton City)

Each state has different rules on whether utility records are public records. For example, Florida, Georgia, South Carolina, and North Carolina consider a person's utility records as public records.

"Third party doctrine," words told to another person, informant, agent, gave police access to documents in the past such as phone, bank, cell phone, hotel records. Utility records were treated similarly, leaving room for smart meter records abuse.

Hackers could easily capture data from the outside with a hand-held device, sell the information to the highest bidder, or establish patterns in order to rob the house.

A court warrant should be required to access the data but neither the Supreme Court nor any lower federal court has ruled on the use of smart meters.

Utilities may sell or share data obtained from smart meters with others in order to increase revenues. Utilities are monopolies and customers cannot switch providers in order to avoid the invasion of privacy.

Electricity is a necessary component of modern life. In some states, customers who removed the smart meters and replaced them with analog meters had their electricity cut off, particularly in California and Nevada. I have watched in humanitarian dismay a video from a meeting with the board of supervisors in California who were pleading with the utilities company to restore power to the home of a 72 year old lady who needed refrigeration for her medicine. The utility company was unmoved by her tears. One home in Nevada has been without electricity for three months because the owner dared to hire a contractor to replace her smart meter with an analog one because the wireless device was making her too sick.

"Advancement of technology threatens to erode further the constitutional protection of privacy." Individuals face a higher risk that activities inside their homes will be monitored by the government. (Congressional Research Service)

Perhaps people should think twice before they accept the $100 check offered by their utility companies in order to "save the planet" and reduce electric bills. Ask the Californians who have filed a class-action lawsuit against PG&E after smart meters were installed and their electric bills have skyrocketed. Is a small $100 bribe meant to help you or hurt you in the long run?

The Drone Attached to Your House

Once a week I check with bated breath my conventional meter attached to the side of my house. I want to make sure no smart meter had been installed in my absence and without my permission. I have written to my utility company that I do not wish to have a smart meter installed, I mailed the letter return receipt requested to make sure that they cannot claim non-receipt. I called the utility office and again, voiced my desire to keep my conventional meter. I received a form letter, telling me that there are no plans yet, smart meters are safe, and there is no opt out, please check the website. I posted a large sign by my conventional meter that they do not have my permission to install a smart meter. When the meter is read, the sign disappears or I find it in the grass. I seem to fight the monopolistic goliath who is the only provider of power.

More and more people who had been harmed by electromagnetic pulses are taking action against their utility company across the nation. Texans Against Smart Meters are considering a class action lawsuit in reference to Fourth Amendment rights violation and health issues commenced or exacerbated by the installation of the Advance Metering System, better known as smart meters.

Smart meter removal from one's home is not enough. Within a five square mile area there is a collecting point of information from all meters and a transmitter receives information from all the collecting points within 125 miles of its location. This transmitter sends all the collected data to a master location, the "mother ship" where everyone's information is stored, analyzed, and sold to a third party who is interested in the household's pattern of usage, consumption of electricity, or possibly "illegal" activity in that home.

During peak usage, the utility company can turn off the power, adjust the thermostat from afar, or turn off entire grid in an "emergency" such as the catastrophic failure of power during the 2012 D.C/Maryland/Virginia straight line winds.

Cyber-attacks and solar flares can also take down an entire section of the smart grid with its smart meters. A person, who wishes to know when the homeowner is at work or on vacation in order to rob the place, can steal the streaming data from the smart meter (which pulses information several times a minute) by standing outside the home with a handheld device.

Louis Donovan of Carson, CA described his heart and pacemaker disruptions from electromagnetic radiation (EMR) emitted by his smart meter which stopped his heart 4 times. (http://www.youtube.com/watch?v=BRDhogkdxW4&list=UUklG6 ilxW_PeYeDSpKSRGZQ)

Abstracts of articles explained the link of low-level microwave radiation and other frequency ranges of radiation exposure to the development of tumors, to DNA (genotoxicity), to production of stress proteins, to heart disturbances, to general brain effects, to blood brain barrier and nerve effects, to immune reactions, and to general functional impairment. (http://articlesofhealth.blogspot.ca/2012/01/adverse-health-effects-from.html)

De-Kun Li, senior researcher at Kaiser Permanente in Oakland, CA, had shown that EMF exposure in the womb is linked to increased risk in childhood obesity. (http://microwavenews.com/news-center/emf-exposures-womb-can-lead-childhood-obesity)

In Hawaii, an electrical contractor in Kauai "recorded a smart meter pulse at a business with emissions more than 1300% than KIUC's claim." Josh de Sol said, "emissions over a 24 hour period, amount to 3.2 hours of exposure to modulated microwave frequency radiation at over 2 milliwatts per square meter which is 240 times greater than what the utility company claims." (http://stopkiuc.com/2012/06/actual-smart-meter-microwave-exposure-video-taped-kapaa-kauai/)

The Maine Supreme Judicial Court ruled on July 12, 2012 that Maine Public Utilities Commission has failed to resolve health and safety issues resulting from the installation of smart meters by Central Maine Power Co. According to Josh Del Sol, opponents to smart meters "argued that utility regulators ignored their legal mandate to ensure the delivery of safe and reasonable utility services." Sadly, the $200 million project, which replaced 615,000 analog meters with smart meters, is complete. Federal stimulus money provided half the cost. The court's decision appeared ineffectual since all smart meters were already installed. (http://www.onlinesentinel.com/news/Law-Court-sides-with-smart-meter-health-issues.html)

Josh Del Sol, producer and director of the movie, Take Back Your Power, writes that "PECO suspended installations of smart meters after local fire officials in Philadelphia attributed them to the cause of several recent home fires." (http://www.phillyburbs.com/news/local/courier_times_news/peco -energy-suspends-installations-of-smart-meters/article_77a2f97c-2e21-590a-b9bb-5468b487b008.html)

To make matters worse, it was discovered that smart meters lack UL and CSA approval and safety testing. "UL has developed a standardized set of safety requirements for utility meters, including smart meters. Even though there are standards, and UL says utilities need to ensure testing, no utility to date (that we know of) has been able to provide evidence of any UL or CSA certification, or accredited safety testing." (Josh del Sol)

UL, according to their website, is a global independent safety science company offering expertise across five areas: product safety, environment, life and health, verification services, and knowledge services.

CSA is a global provider of product testing and certification services for US, Canada and countries worldwide for many products and components.

People should be gravely concerned that utilities have installed and are installing at a rapid pace the untested, unapproved device called smart meter which controls all electrical usage, causes fires, and serious health effects. On my recent trip to Europe, I photographed banks of smart meters everywhere, installed with European Union funds.

Josh del Sol described the interview with John Horgan, New Democrat Party Energy Critic in British Columbia. Del Sol asked him why British Columbia Hydro is installing unapproved devices. His answer was, "I don't know... I don't know. It's mind-numbing, isn't it?"

We do know why utilities are installing smart meters in the U.S. – it is a convenient way to control our energy use and thus our independence by using the ruse of convenience, modernization, cheaper energy, expedience, and better service. Nothing can be further from the truth. Smart meters are convenient ways to spy on the populace, charge them more per kilowatt hour of consumption, reduce consumption by cutting power delivery, control the population and its health, reduce costs for utilities who no longer have to worry about storage capacity and building additional storage plants which are expensive, reducing costs of wire maintenance under and above ground, and eliminating meter readers for conventional meters.

The UN Agenda 21 Marches on with the USDA-EPA Partnership

John Adams said, "Property must be secured, or liberty cannot exist." The Decalogue emphasized private property in "Thou shalt not steal." George Washington stated, "Private property and freedom are inseparable."

Private property was so important to our Founding Fathers that its principles were included in the Declaration of Independence, the Constitution, and the Bill of Rights. The right to property is surmised in the owner's determination of land use, as long as its use does not "disturb the equal rights of another."

The Declaration of Independence states that "...all Men...are endowed by their Creator with Certain unalienable Rights, that among these are Life, Liberty, and the Pursuit of Happiness." United Nations Charter and Declaration of Human Rights are based on the idea that rights are granted and rescinded by men. The UN third world nations planners devised Agenda 21 on three suspect principles: Equity, Economy, and Environment, all controlled by government because "individual rights must take a back seat to the collective."

In 1964, UN developing nations called for the establishment of a **New International Economic Order**, asking that multi-national corporations be regulated, foreign property nationalized, asking to establish commodity monopolies, and requesting transfer of technology and technical assistance.

Developed nations ignored this declaration but developing nations promoted these ideas at other conferences. In 1976, **the Conference on Human Settlements (Habitat One)** declared that private land ownership and wealth are the primary reasons for *social injustice.* The 65 page socialist document recommended land use:

- Redistribution of population in accordance with resources
- Government must control the use of land in order to achieve equitable distribution of resources
- Land use must be controlled through zoning and planning
- Government must control excessive profits from land use
- Urban and rural land reform should be done through public ownership of land
- Public authorities should hold developing rights of land and should be separated from owner rights

The 1987 UN report, "Our Common Future" by the World Commission on Environment and Development focused on the policy of **sustainable development**: land use, education, and population control and reduction. **Sustainable Development** made nature and its protection the central principle for all member nations.

The 1992 **UN Bruntland Commission** released the official **UN Agenda 21** with its 40 chapters and the 178 nations who signed and agreed to implement UN Agenda 21 at the conference in Rio de Janeiro. Signatory for the United States was President George H. W. Bush.

All countries agreed that decisions must be made based on how they will affect the environment. Property is evil and creates wealth for the rich at the expense of the poor. Business is evil, should be controlled by the community, while the owner is responsible, and pays taxes. Wealth was produced at the expense of the poor and must thus be confiscated and given to the poor. No private enterprise should exist, only **public-private partnerships**. These ideas are tenets of socialism/Marxism.

UN Agenda 21 set out to abolish private property, control education, control and reduce population, and control the economy. The global plan was called **Sustainable Development**.

Every one of the 40 chapters contains policies that member nations must adopt such as demographics, settlements, sustainable communities, water control, land use control, role of business, energy control, role of industry, international mechanisms of implementing the agenda, and the institutions used to implement the policies.

In 1993, President Bill Clinton signed the **Biodiversity Treaty.** The treaty was used to implement UN Agenda 21 in the United States, "Creation of national strategies, plans, policies, and processes which are crucial in achieving a sustainable world."

Dr. Michael Coffman revealed a map to the U.S. Senate of the proposed development of the **Wildlands** under UN Agenda 21 in the U.S. This map had red, yellow, and green zones noted as Core Reserves and Corridors with little or no human use, Buffer Zones with highly regulated use, and Smart Growth with human settlements.

http://www.mtmultipleuse.org/wilderness/wildlands_map.htm

President Clinton signed Executive Order 12852, creating the **President's Council on Sustainable Development** to translate UN Agenda 21 into public policy administered by the federal government. The Council created the first UN Agenda 21 called "Sustainable America," with 16 "we believe" statements. The ultimate goals were to abolish private property, control education, control and reduce population, and control the economy.

To aid in implementing UN Agenda 21 a *Consensus Process* was developed: *Stakeholders* of the *Affected Group* select an *Initiator* who then selects a *Decision-Making Committee* (steering committee); *Policy Decisions* are pre-determined by a *Facilitator* and not by the Committee (they cannot vote). *Consensus* is the process in which objections to the proposal are erased. The *Affected Group* has to abide by the pre-determined decision with no voice in choosing the decision-maker or the outcome.

President's Council on Sustainable Development (PCSD) published "Sustainable America, a New Consensus," which contains 150 policy recommendations taken directly from UN Agenda 21. Secretary of Commerce Ron Brown said that his agency could implement 67 percent of the recommendations administratively, using rule-making authority.

Land Management Agencies promoted land use policies based on ecological or aesthetic consequences. The agencies appropriated millions in grants to state and local governments and set up land trusts for the purpose of acquiring private property. For example, by 1997, 43 million acres were designated roadless areas, 1/3 of land in America was owned by government and ten percent by states, 21 national monuments were expanded. (Donna Holt)

How was UN Agenda 21 implemented at the grass roots? Millions in grants were awarded to state and local governments by American Planning Association and EPA through "visioning."

A *Visioning Council* (steering committee) made up of businessmen, politicians, NGOs (non-governmental organizations), and people who stood to gain financially from the implementation of the goals of UN Agenda 21, worked with the EPA, the American Planning Association, the Conservation Fund, the National Resources Defense Council, and the Sierra Club.

The Visioning Council received their proposal from the President's Council on Sustainable Development (PCSD) and proposed it as local goals for the community. The *"consensus"* would remove any objections the public may have had. The result was the **"vision"** and the new plan of action. The entire process took 12-18 months.

The Initiator would make press releases to introduce the idea of Sustainable Communities and to build huge public support; the elected officials signed on without any questions asked. They either did not understand the nefarious intent or were financially complicit in the "vision." Some local government officials had no idea that the plan came from the United Nations Agenda 21.

Examples of partners of Sustainable Development are ICLEI, International County/City Management Association, American Planning Association, Renaissance Planning Group, and Florida Forever (largest public land acquisition program in the U.S. – 9.8 million acres purchased). They provide technical support and assistance with SD, management training, performance measurement, rural and urban planning.

According to Donna Holt's data, in June 2008, **The One Planet Communities** proposed the following:

- 58 percent less electricity
- 65 percent vehicle mileage down time
- 23 gallons/water less per person
- 50 percent reduction in car ownership
- 40 electric car solar powered charging stations

- Reduction of footprint from 6 homes to 2 homes by 2020
- Stacked homes to avoid expansion of housing developments
- Five minute lifestyle (5 minute walk or bike from your home to shop, work, live, school)
- Walk or bike within the community
- Car-sharing for short distances or from one stacked community to another
- High speed rail for longer distances
- Car ownership will disappear
- UN Agenda 21-driven on-going developments, indoctrination, laws, and industry regulation have profound consequences in our country
- Sustainability is taught k-12, colleges, and universities
- Colleges teach how to "build earth's sustainable workforce," "sustainability manager for carbon accounting," "corporate sustainability manager," "energy auditor," "engineering sustainably certified homes," to name just a few
- Children are well indoctrinated into Sustainable Development practices
- Government schemes to control future use of agricultural land and water through the recently passed White House Rural Council
- San Joaquin Valley in California was turned into a virtual dust bowl when water was denied to farmers in order to protect the delta smelt; 40,000 people became unemployed; less vegetables and fruits resulted in higher prices
- Regulatory taking of land, especially in Florida, Miami-Dade County
- Rationing of water, electricity, and fuel
- Expensive retrofitting of homes – people will be forced to leave their homes if they cannot afford the expensive retrofitting
- Denied building permits and thus land is deemed worthless
- Private property abolished to prevent urban sprawl
- Land shortage
- High density living
- Megacities regionalism will replace local and state governments

In June 2011, President Obama signed the White House Rural Council. To make good on the promise to control rural life and its resources, on August 8, 2011, the U.S. Department of Agriculture and the EPA announced a national partnership "to improve rural drinking water and wastewater systems."

The Secretary of Agriculture, Tom Vilsack, who chairs the White House Rural Council that controls 16% of U.S. land, "is working to coordinate USDA programs across the government and encourage public-private partnerships, to improve economic conditions and create jobs in rural communities." Having finished "saving or creating three million jobs" in urban areas, the government has now moved into rural areas. Here is UN Agenda 21 in action through its hallmark public-private partnerships, to "fundamentally change" and control the use of water, resources, and agricultural land.

The Battles on the UN Agenda 21 Front

As the battles against the green sustainability monster pushed by ICLEI and Non-Governmental Organizations (NGOs) rage across the nation, twenty communities and counting have officially rejected membership in the International Council for Local Environmental Initiatives (ICLEI).

Legislators across the nation have introduced bills to reject anything proposed and promoted by UN Agenda 21.

Rep. Matt Shay reported the creation of an anti-UN Agenda 21 Caucus in the Washington State Legislature.

The Wisconsin Legislature has introduced two bills (Assembly Bill 303 and Senate Bill 225) to "allow local governments to repeal comprehensive development plans that were forced under smart growth legislation." "The bill eliminates the grant program that was set up to finance the smart growth planning."(Tom De Weese, The American Policy Center)

The GOP platform of the Republican National Convention in Tampa rejected the United Nation's Agenda 21 scheme as a threat to national sovereignty. They also rejected any global tax or other controversial programs promoted by the United Nations.

The joint, non-binding resolution HJR 587 passed both the House and the Senate in Tennessee in March 2012 opposing UN Agenda 21 and its globalist encroachment on liberty.

The academia constantly promotes UN Agenda 21 and indoctrinates students into subscribing to the idea of a global planet overseen by the few and very wise elites.

The Office of Sustainability Institute at George Mason University invited the "sustainability community" of Fairfax, Virginia, to the **Sustainable Living Roadshow** on October 19, 2011. If you had no clue about the nature of this road show, it would be safe to guess, it is environmental propaganda. I am still trying to understand the need for a sustainability institute at GMU but then every government entity now has such an office or at least a sustainability plan.

When I saw the invitation, I began to understand the depth and length of brainwashing that the environmental minority is assaulting this country with in order to pass and promote their anti-American agenda.

"The Sustainable Living Roadshow is a caravan of educators and entertainers who tour the country in a fleet of renewable fuel vehicles setting up off-the-grid eco-carnivals with interactive learning villages at K-12 schools, universities, festivals and community events. These villages are designed to empower communities to utilize sustainable living strategies for a healthier planet."

The sponsors of the Sustainable Living Roadshow are an interesting mixture of corporations, stores, and environmental groups: Birkenstock, Nature's Gate, Petzl, Hemp Oil Canada, Organic India, The Living Seed Company, Hemp Industries Association, Elemental Herbs, Natracare, and Synchro. (www.sustainablelivingroadshow.org)

The Sustainable Living Roadshow website displayed pictures of energetic young people holding signs that read, "Toss out fossil fuels," "We're Ready, Green Jobs Now," emphasizing a global culture, another element of UN Agenda 21, a powerful assault on impressionable minds to erase any trace of our culture, our nationality, our borders, our sovereignty.

Young people are easily swayed by rhetoric, clever and deceptive advertising, art, influential teachers, TV shows, and brainwashing done by such roadshows. Take for instance art, art craftily named Roboknitters. The Dutch artist Marijke Vijfhuizen used two robotic arms knitting blue garbage bags into a plastic blanket covering a green field of grass as a metaphor for the growing ecological burden of consumerism. This is her idea of using a visually arresting medium to influence what young people should believe about consumerism and pollution.

It does not matter that there is no viable and economical full replacement for fossil fuels yet to run the largest economy on the planet. Let us toss them out because teachers and environmentalists say so. There is no green industry and there are no green jobs. Students, impressionable children, and ignorant adults have overlooked these tiny details. The media never reports the truth. People do not know that there are no green jobs and no green industry, just wind turbines and solar panels.

GMU asked attendees to arrive preferably by bike or public transportation, keeping in line with their walkability and mass-transit goals, which happen to coincide with UN Agenda 21. My very wise mother mumbled that they must be out of their minds if they think that Americans would abandon their cars willingly for mass transit or walking.

I wondered if parents knew what kind of brain washing their expensive tuition bought for their children and what kind of generation was going to lead our country into the future.

As universities and government agencies across the country were busy brainwashing our children, young people and adults into UN Agenda 21 Smart Growth and Livability in order to save the planet, the National Center for Policy Analysis was busy testing the claims made by the "Green" movement.(ncpa.org)

If you asked any environmental group or government agency pushing UN Agenda 21, they would tell you that moving to higher density areas, walking, biking, taking mass transit five minutes from work was the solution to urban sprawl and destruction of the planet.

Environmental groups prefer that forests be kept pristine and roadless, giving back to wilderness as many acres as possible. Bill Clinton passed the 2001 Roadless Area Conservation Rule which was upheld on October 21, 2011 by the Denver-based U.S. Tenth Circuit Court of Appeals via a 120-page ruling. The rule was issued to protect nearly 60 million acres of America's national forests and grasslands. There can be no road-building or commercial timber harvesting on large remaining roadless areas around the country.

Crowding humans off their lands and off their suburban homes into high-density, high-rise mixed-use tenements, on the other hand, is a desirable policy of those who support "smart growth" and "livability."

Urban planners and public officials have been pushing the idea that "smart growth" and "livability" in denser urban areas would lead to lower levels of air pollution primarily because of reduction in travel by car.

EPA data show "higher population densities to be strongly associated with higher levels of automobile travel and more concentrated air pollution emissions."

Data from 425 counties with major metropolitan areas (1 million or more in population) show nitrogen oxides (NOx) emissions in 2008. Seven of the ten counties with the highest nitrogen oxides emissions concentration (annual tons per square mile) were also the top 10 in population density.

Manhattan in New York County had the most intense nitrogen oxides emissions and the densest population. Manhattan had highest concentration in other air pollutants, carbon monoxide, particulates, and volatile organic compounds. Bronx, Kings, and Queens were also more densely populated counties and among the top ten in NOx emissions. (ncpa.org)

"More concentrated traffic leads to greater traffic congestion and more intense air pollution. The data for traffic concentration is similar to population density. Counties with the greatest density of traffic are also counties with the highest population density."

Counties with more than 20,000 people per square mile have 14 times the concentration of NOx than the average county and motor vehicle travel is 22 times higher than the average. Sierra Club and ICLEI, strong supporters of densification, researched and found that traffic volume increased with density. (ncpa.org)

EPA air pollution regulation was implemented with the idea to safeguard public health and reduce health risks. Densification worsens traffic, air pollution, and increases health risks, defeating efforts to meet federal standards. Case in point, Tampa-St. Petersburg metro area might not meet the new federal standards. The solution proposed is densification, more "Smart Growth" and "Livability" which will likely worsen air pollution and health risks. (Wendell Cox)

The policy of "smart growth" and "livability," moving people into high density, mixed-used tenements in urban areas within five minutes walk or bike from school, work, and shopping, forcing people out of their cars and into public transportation actually causes higher housing prices, higher cost of living, "muted" economic growth, decreased mobility, decreased access to jobs, increased air pollution, increased traffic congestion, and increased health risks. http://demographia.com/db-countynox.pdf

Global Warming Crowd Opposed
in Virginia

After global warming was debunked, omniscient environmentalists changed their rhetoric to global cooling and now to climate-change. Of course, the climate has been changing back and forth for thousands of years without human input, but environmentalists have now noticed because it justifies their man as culprit agenda. How else could a minority impose their omnipotent will on the majority?

Because 30,000 readings of temperatures around the globe have shown the earth as cooling since 1997, Al Gore and his supporters have changed their talking points from global warming to climate-change.

Record-low temperatures in parts of Eastern Europe caused death tolls from Ukraine to Romania. Two meters of snow covered villages and towns in Romania, such as Buzau, forcing occupants to leave their homes through the roof. Mountains of snow trapped people in their homes and many were feared dead. The waters of the Black Sea froze quite a distance from the shore. Wave protection dams froze in the port of Constanta.

In the meantime, in Virginia, the Middle Peninsula Planning District Commission was making municipal preparations for sea-level rise caused by climate change. According to the Washington Post, "a well-organized and vocal group of residents has taken a keen interest" in the proceedings, opposing planners and politicians who promote man-made global warming.

"The residents' opposition has focused on a central point: They don't think climate change is accelerated by human activity, as most climate scientists conclude." (Washington Post)

The truth is that most scientists do not conclude that climate change is caused or accelerated by human activity. One thousand scientists, some of whom had received the Nobel Prize in science, took a one-page ad in the Washington Post stating their disagreement with the faux proclamations of global warming.

Darryl Fears described the Middle Peninsula area as having "historic geological issues." "A meteor landed nearby 35 million years ago, creating the Chesapeake Bay Impact Crater. In addition, a downward-pressing glacial formation was created during the Ice Age. These ancient events are causing the land to sink, accounting for about one-third of the sea-level change, scientists say."

Municipal planners redesigned the area as a future flood zone. Officials, who use name-calling to discredit the opposition, called the citizens against the plan, "activists acting on a hoax." The hoax in question is UN Agenda 21.

"Agenda 21 is the least thing they should be worried about," said Patty Glick, senior climate-change specialist for the National Wildlife Federation, "It has no legal or policy implications for local governments in the United States." Yet 600 communities around the U.S. are members of the International Council on Local Environmental Initiatives (ICLEI), the implementation organization of UN Agenda 21.

According to Shereen Hughes, a former planning commissioner in James City County, "The uprising against smart growth is ridiculous and a conspiracy theory imagined by fear mongers."

"In Gloucester County, planners sat stone-faced as activists took turns reading portions of the 500-page UN Agenda 21 text, delaying a meeting for more than an hour." (Washington Post)

As usual, progressives find the opposition of conservative citizens annoying because they object to smart growth plans that Americans never voted on or agreed to.

"Agenda 21 is an agenda in name only," environmentalists say. If UN Agenda 21 is a "conspiracy theory," then environmentalists are spending vast fortunes and UN resources trying to implement it across the globe, with conferences attended by thousands of delegates from 179 countries.

If UN Agenda 21 is a figment of the "Agenders'" imagination, why did President Clinton sign Executive Order 12852, creating the President's Council on Sustainable Development to translate UN Agenda 21 into public policy administered by the federal government? Why did the President's Council create the first "Sustainable America" with 16 'we believe' statements with the end goal to abolish private property, control education, control and reduce population, and control the economy?

In the absence of a global treaty to reduce carbon dioxide emissions, a gas that plants need to grow, environmentalists have now switched to two other possible shorter-term culprits that "drive climate change," methane and soot, also called black carbons.

The suggestion to slow global warming is simple, say Brian Vastag and Juliet Eilperin, "to get people in Uganda and India to adopt cleaner-burning stoves," and to convince farmers in third world countries to plow agricultural waste under instead of burning it. Could we also cork volcanoes from burping ash, CO_2, and other gases into the atmosphere and on the ocean floor?

According to Washington Post, computer simulations by a 24-member international team claim, "reducing methane and soot would slow global warming dramatically – by almost a degree Fahrenheit – by the middle of the century." I am skeptical of this precision since meteorology science cannot even accurately predict what the temperatures will be tomorrow.

U.S. has spent $60 million to support methane reduction projects overseas and pledged $50 million more, including $5 million to the Arctic Council Initiative to reduce black carbon emissions in Russia. (Emily Cain, State Department)

"Environmentalists have always had an agenda to put nature above man. If they can find an end to their means, they do not care how it happens. If they can do it under the guise of global warming and climate change, they will do it." (Donna Holt, Virginia Campaign for Liberty)

Chantell and Mike Sackett's dream house in the Idaho Panhandle had become the latest battleground against the EPA and the enforcement of the Clean Water Act. According to developers, corporations, utilities, libertarians, and conservative members of

Congress, their fight had become a prime example of the EPA's "abominable bureaucratic abuse."

The Supreme Court decided on the four-year battle (Sackett v. EPA) over the 0.63-acre lot, located in a subdivision with sewer hookup, a lot deemed wetlands by the EPA. The EPA does have an "important environmental mandate which we don't deny, but the agency is out of control and has been for some time." Fortunately, the Sacketts prevailed.(Damien M. Schiff, the Pacific Legal Foundation)

Whether it is EPA onerous powers over wetlands or environmentalists affecting local planning and redesigning properties as flood zones, we are fighting a war against federal regulations and against the implementation of UN Agenda 21 mandates.

Anthropocene - Age of Man

If you have not seen this word, it is because it was invented by the global warming crowd, supported by United Nations Agenda 21's goal of total global control through environmental protection policies that will fundamentally alter the way humans exist.

According to a National Geographic article published in March 2011, "Age of Man," the word "anthropocene" was conceived ten years ago by the Dutch chemist Paul Crutzen who said, "we are no longer in the Holocene, we are in the Anthropocene." The Holocene was the period between the last ice age, 11,500 years ago, and present time. Paul Crutzen received a Nobel Prize for the discovery of ozone-depleting compounds. (Elizabeth Kolbert)

Antonio Stoppani suggested "anthropozoic" term in 1870 but was derided as unscientific. There was no global warming crowd then with a population control agenda to give it credence. The term "Anthropocene" was welcome because it fit in with the Malthusian style theory of population growth overwhelming the planet and eventually causing its demise. According to E. O. Wilson, the seven billion people have increased the biomass "a hundred times larger than any other large animal species that has ever walked the Earth." (Elizabeth Kolbert)

The April 1, 2012 issue of the journal "Earth and Planetary Science" published a study by a team from Syracuse University in New York which found that the "Medieval Warm Period" of approximately 500 to 1,000 years ago extended to Antarctica. (Mail Online)

The lead geochemist Zunli Lu found reliable evidence to study past temperature changes and climate conditions in a rare mineral, "ikaite." "Ikaite is an icy version of limestone, said Lu. Ikaite is stable in cold conditions and melts at room temperature."

The "Little Ice Age" (which lasted from 1300 to 1850) and the "Medieval Warm Period" were climate events documented in Northern Europe via crystals found in earth's layers. Lu and his team were able to ascertain that these two events reached Antarctica because they found and studied heavy oxygen isotopes in the ikaite crystals. "The water that holds the crystal structure together – called hydration water – traps information about temperatures present when the crystals formed." (Ted Thornhill)

The Intergovernmental Panel on Climate Change (IPCC), established by the United Nations Environment Programme (UNEP), is still arguing that the "Medieval Warm Period" was limited to Europe.

Common Dreams.org, with its motto "Building Progressive Community," published an article on March 27, 2012, "On the Brink: Planet Near Irreversible Point of Global Warming." It did not matter that global warming alarmists and scientists had been shamed publicly for having hidden or erased the scientific data that proved them wrong. They are marching on with their agenda. The "sky is falling" scientists at the "Planet under Pressure" conference in London said, "we may have already passed the tipping points on global warming."

Martin Rees of the Royal Society said, "this century is the first when one species – ours – has the planet's future in its hands." It is embarrassing to read that humans are so omnipotent that we have God-like powers.

Reuter's Agency reported that "global warming is close to becoming irreversible," world temperatures are going to rise 6 degrees by 2100. It is shocking that they can predict with such accuracy and clarity what will happen 100 years from now when they cannot even predict weather accurately for tomorrow.

"Man's catastrophic damage to the environment and disparities between rich and poor head the daunting challenges facing the Rio +20 Summit in June, experts said. The summit must sweep away a system that lets reckless growth destroy the planet's health yet fails to help billions in need." (Agency France Presse)

Therein lies the true intent of the global warming scam and the United Nations Agenda 21 – fleecing developed nations, spreading the wealth to developing nations, population control, energy control, economic control, education control, confiscation of private property, control of the seas, commerce, military, and de-growing the biggest "offender," the United States, to a primitive lifestyle.

The educational propaganda is getting more intense. Planet under Pressure has commissioned a 3-minute film "from the start of the industrial revolution to the Rio +20 Summit," the world's first educational web portal on the **Anthropocene**. The film exaggerates the growth of humanity in the last 250 years into such a global force "on an equivalent scale to major geological processes."

This film is outrageous, yet it will become part of our children's education in the classroom. Parents will have no idea that the movie will be shown to their children, just like the video, "The Story of Stuff," which distorts capitalism and promotes socialism.

The facts that the planet has corrected itself and human/non-human intervention or occupation had no significant bearing, are ignored in the "logic" of environmentalists. Older and moneyed "greens" have brainwashed our children into Save the Planet activism through intense and expensive propaganda - evil humans are destroying Earth through careless existence and breathing. The planet has always been here and it will be here long after we are gone. We do not need to return to primitive lifestyles in order to please "greenies" and their tyrannical agendas.

Every school has encouraged students to turn off their lights for one hour in honor of Earth Day, an event that is insignificant in terms of energy saved or "carbon foot print reduction," as recognized by environmentalists themselves. It is a symbolic attempt to brainwash students into believing that we are destroying the planet deliberately by using energy and by our mere existence.

Liberals do not seem to care that, if there is no coal, there is little electricity and no electric cars. If there is no oil, there is no energy, gasoline, cars, heat, air conditioning, travel, mobility, and other modern conveniences.

Secretary of Energy Chu wants us to pay $50 for a bulb. Edison's incandescent and inexpensive bulb that has served humanity well for so long is passé. How many bulbs does the average household have, times $50? Can we afford such expensive bulbs or the mercury-emitting CFL variety, which also poison the immediate environment with mercury when broken? My answer is a resounding no. We must stand up to United Nations and to homegrown environmentalists' quest to de-grow America, control our lives, and impose their "vision" of the world on the majority.

Rio +20 Earth Summit

The United Nations is not giving up its assault on the economic and political future of our country and of our planet. The first installment of United Nations to control the globe environmentally and economically was "UN Conference on Environment and Development (UNCED)," held in Rio in 1992. The UN Brundtland Commission released its official UN Agenda 21 that same year, following the Conference on Human Settlements in 1976 and the 1987 report, "Our Common Future."

The 1992 conference in Rio produced three documents and a tropical forest agreement which was limited to a few nations:

-   UN Framework Convention on Climate Change (an international treaty)
-   UN Convention on Biological Diversity (an international treaty)
-   Agenda 21 (not a treaty)

The UN Framework Convention on Climate Change was initially voluntary compliance but was changed into a legally binding treaty with the 1997 Kyoto Protocol. The U.S. ratified the first treaty but not the Kyoto Protocol.

President Bush did not sign the UN Convention on Biological Diversity because it was legally binding and required transfer of technology without recognizing proprietary rights. The full Senate scheduled a vote after the Senate Foreign Relations Committee passed the Convention on Biological Diversity by a vote of 16-3 on June 29, 1994. One hour before the vote, the "treaty" was pulled from the schedule. (Henry Lamb)

The policy of Sustainable Development, land use, education, population control and reduction, made nature and its protection the central principle for all member nations.

The 65-page socialist document released from the Conference on Human Settlements (1976) declared private land ownership and wealth as primary reasons for "social injustice." Its recommendations that were later incorporated in UN Agenda 21 are:

- Redistribution of population according to resources
- Government control of land use in order to achieve equitable distribution of resources
- Land use control through zoning and planning
- Government control of excessive profits from land use
- Urban and rural land control through public land ownership
- Developing rights must be held by public authorities

The United States, represented by President Bush, signed part 1 and part 3 of the Rio's UN Conference on Environment and Development in 1992. One hundred seventy-eight other nations signed the conference documents that proposed regulations, organizations, and practices that limit the economic behavior of citizens, organizations, and firms with regard to water use, land use, transfer of technology, and human habitation under global governance.

The 40 chapters of the U.N. Agenda 21 signed in 1992 in Rio is not really a treaty, "It is a soft-law document." The nations whose representatives signed the document were "morally obligated to implement them, according to the United Nations." (Henry Lamb)

Because the recommendations were not legally binding under Agenda 21, strongly suggested regulations were implemented administratively, bypassing Congress. Congress has not debated nor adopted UN Agenda 21, yet certain provisions have been included in law from time to time such as Senator Dodd's "Livable Communities Act."

Agenda 21 recommendations are converted into law at the local level as they are incorporated into Comprehensive Land Use Plans which are adopted and included into local zoning codes.

President Clinton signed Executive Order 12852, creating the President's Council on Sustainable Development to translate UN Agenda 21 into U.S. public policy called "ecosystem management," administered by the federal government.

The President's Council created "Sustainable America" with 16 "we believe" statements. The ultimate goals were to abolish private property, control education, control and reduce population, and control the economy. Currently, every federal government agency has a sustainable UN Agenda 21 plan. (www.fedcenter.gov)

The charade was played again in Brazil – "Rio +20 United Nations Conference on Sustainable Development," twenty years later. The conference was titled, "The Future We Want." Who is "We?" Most Americans do not dream such a future.

During June 20-22, 2012, participants signed on to 10 new sustainable development goals for the planet and promised to build a global green economy in order to reduce consumption and poverty. (The Guardian)

Countries agreed to protect oceans against overfishing, to publish and approve an annual state of the planet report, to subscribe to a single world agency for the environment, and to appoint a Global High Commissioner for Future Generations or "ombudsperson."

Stephen Hale, Oxfam's deputy advocacy and campaigns director, wanted the Rio negotiations to develop "concrete proposals on sustainable agriculture and food security."

Ruth Davis, chief policy advisor of Greenpeace, UK, wanted an end to "the wild-west plundering of the high seas." Was she referring to Somali pirates? I am still in awe how they can count creatures per cubic foot in the oceans when they are constantly in motion. Do they police fishing themselves or do they depend on voluntary reporting of each fishing vessel?

The overfishing would end if everyone would ratify The Convention on the Law of the Sea (LOST) as the Obama administration desires. Member nations would surrender sovereignty over their territorial seas once they voluntarily agree to act according to the treaty and "other rules of international law." (Henry Lamb)

The UN bemoaned in its Rio +20 draft the setbacks in food insecurity, climate change, biodiversity loss, the existence of 1.4 billion people who live in extreme poverty and one-sixth under-nourished, pandemics, and epidemics. "Unsustainable development has increased the stress on the earth's limited natural resources and on the carrying capacity of ecosystems. Our planet supports seven billion people expected to be 9 billion by 2050."

"We emphasize the importance of culture for sustainable development. We call for a holistic approach to sustainable development which will guide humanity to live in harmony with nature."

The United Nations Rio +20 conference in June 2012 demanded:

- Universal access and right to information and communications technology
- Poverty eradication
- Integration of local governments into all levels of decision making in sustainable development
- The need to reflect the views of children and youth
- No new trade barriers
- No new conditions on aid and finance
- No subsidies
- Green technology in the public domain for all to share
- Global policy framework requiring all listed and large private companies to integrate sustainability information within UN required reporting cycles
- Move the entire world to low-carbon development
- The UN-established specialized agency for the environment with universal membership located in Nairobi, Kenya
- Regular review of the state of the planet and Earth's carrying capacity
- Global trade should be regulated by World Bank, International Monetary Fund, World Trade Organization, and regional development banks
- Development and implementation of integrated water resource management
- Efficient human settlements (there is something scary about the phrase "human settlements," it has a negative and frightening quality)

- Restoration and enhancement of natural capital
- Sustainable land and water management practices
- Family farming, ecological farming, organic production systems
- Sustainable forest management
- Rational use of biodiversity for economic purposes
- New markets linked to renewable and unconventional energy sources
- Green job creation/green economy
- Promote education for sustainable development

It looks like the "greenologists" and the third world dictators at the UN have a lot of work to do, determining how to better steal our wealth, technology, to indoctrinate impressionable youth into the religion of Gaia, and replenish their bank accounts with U.S., western money, and economic aid under the "wise" United Nations global governance and the guise of eradicating poverty.

Green, Rotten, and Red
Sustainability Indoctrination

Every day I step outside my house I am reminded that every person born in this country is an American but not every American is a patriot. A patriot contributes to America's exceptionalism, making it a better place for all. Americans rebuild what others have destroyed without propaganda and grants from the government.

Real Americans defend freedom around the world and do not apologize for their kindness, generosity of time, treasure, sweat, and blood. Real Americans love their country and wish to protect and preserve the land and waters they have inherited from Americans before us so that our children and grandchildren can enjoy it free of any interference from government, foreign powers, or United Nations.

Then there are those Americans who think our society is an "unjust" society. They are usually the brain washed, trust fund beneficiaries, who have never had to live under the "socially-just" utopian societies they so desire. They've never had to be subjected to the indignities of communism in Cuba, Russia, North Korea, Iran, and other dictatorships they consider "paradise." With every breath they take, these Americans want to fundamentally change our society to their desires and their terribly misplaced dreams that the rest of America loathes and despises. These are the "green environmentalists," the "non-profits" who want to shape, influence, and change your consumer choices via "green options."

You don't have to take my word, just visit the Green Festival in Washington, D.C., September 29-30, 2012, a project of **Green America: Economic Action for a Just Planet** (http://www.greenamerica.org/) and **Global Exchange** (http://www.globalexchange.org/). Other sponsors include:

Sierra Club (http://www.sierraclub.org/)

Earth Balance (http://www.earthbalance.com/)

Sustainu (http://www.sustainuclothing.com/)

Democracy Now (http://en.wikipedia.org/wiki/Democracy_Now!)

Ford Community Green Grant Ford (http://www.greenfestivals.org/national/ford-community-green-grant-2012-nyc-chicago)

Ford Motors

"Green America is a national nonprofit consumer organization, promoting environmental sustainability, social justice, and economic justice through marketplace." Sustainability, social justice, environmental justice, and economic justice are code words for UN Agenda 21, global communism.

"Global Exchange is an international human rights organization dedicated to promoting social, economic and environmental justice around the world."

No American objects to cleaning and protecting the environment in which we live, and we do not purposefully pollute it, but we must admit that the "greening" of America agenda is really the "reding" of America, turning us finally into a communist country. We are already so socialist, we can only recognize a smidgen of the former capitalist glory.

The Green Festival in D.C. is a "non-profit event, dedicated to celebrating social justice and sharing a vision of a healthier and more just future for us all." I already live in a socially just society with equal opportunity for all citizens. What individual citizens choose to do with their time and the choices they make determine their future. It is not society's responsibility to see that sloth and laziness are rewarded equally to those who work hard to achieve.

Who knew that social justice and a just future involved bicycle maintenance, container gardening, home brewing, recycled crafts, yoga classes, NAACP, Washington Peace Center, 350.org (http://www.350.org/ - 350.org is building a global grassroots movement to solve the non-existent and manufactured climate crisis), local non-profits, and national initiatives to speed up the transformation of America into the UN Agenda 21's idea of one-world communist governance?

Recognizable speakers include consumer advocate Ralph Nader, Congressman Dennis Kucinich, and Medea Benjamin, cofounder of the infamous Code Pink. The 125 progressive speakers tackle topics of sustainable economy, social justice, the expensive and so far often bankrupt green energy, community organizing (where did I hear that term before), Fair Trade, green business, ecological balance, urban farming, healthy home, environmental advocacy, green building, and toxic free living.

Urban farming sounds interesting. The EPA and the federal government are taking more and more land away from agriculture, either confiscating it or paying farmers not to farm, and giving land back to the wilderness but we are supposed to feed 313 million Americans via urban farming from high rise, densely populated tenements in the city?

The orgy of sustainability celebration includes green office, green pets, eco-travel (it must be paddling your own canoe to Europe with a bicycle attached to it), green media, the phantom green jobs that never materialized, eco-arts and crafts, organic food, green building and renovation, and "unbelievable green shopping."

Ford Motors is promoting test driving its new Ford Focus Electric and C-MAX Hybrid. At the same time, Ford is awarding a $5,000 grant for "sustainable, forward-thinking ideas for improving the environment in local communities."

A bike valet is provided if you are still alive after biking for miles to get to D.C. and the traffic did not kill you before exhaustion. Plant-based diet, raw food, raw fruit pie, raising urban chickens (that should be quite smelly and unsanitary), vegan sushi, brew your own "sustainable beer" (you will need to get drunk on that after all the weirdness in your daily life), and vegetarian food demonstrations will teach how to build a vegan pantry. (Do vegans live longer than the rest of us?) Sustainable cats, raw pet diet, how pets can help heal the planet (that is rich), and fashion for 4-paw friends should be interesting.

The festival teaches "how to break up with your bank," changing a flat bike tire, how to be a responsible tourist, and about "electric bikes and the sustainable transportation revolution." Electric bikes must be designed for those who are fat or handicapped and cannot traditionally bike or walk miles to work, grocery store, and school.

It appears that "sustainability can save humanity from itself," create clean energy for all, provide "no stink indoor composting with worms," and help humans to "find fullness: mindful eating." We are so fat and such pigs that we must have the federal government tell us what to eat and when to stop eating.

If you are not that much into having your life changed into sustainable everything, there are other topics at the Green Festival on political agitation, Occupiers, community organizing, AIDS, and voter fraud:

- Billionaires and the Ballot Bandits: the Theft of 2012 --- How the 99% can occupy peace (Medea Benjamin)
- Alternatives to Neo-Liberalism: Latin American Leadership (tin pot dictators as leaders – laughable)
- We can save the world while we are young (Chicken Little, the Sky is Falling)
- Vibrant living: From healthy choices to political action
- Global collapse, prophecies, the future, and you
- One Earth, one people, one nation, one chance (we are global citizens now under one world government, no more pesky borders, sovereignty, language, nationality, culture)
- The silenced majority: Stories of uprisings, occupations, resistance, and hope
- AIDS activism from DC to Durban

If the festival attendance was free of charge, I would love to go for the spectacle component. But I refuse to spend $49 for green schools, green kids, and red Marxist environmental green indoctrination sold as two days of fun.

Martha's Plight and Liberty Farm Under Agenda 21

Fauquier County's Board of Supervisors in Virginia, presumably Republican controlled, passed an ordinance to force wineries to close at 6 p.m. and to prohibit the sale of food unless the wineries obtain special permits from the zoning administrator. They fined Liberty Farm for having a pumpkin carving that never took place and for having a birthday party for eight little girls without proper permit. Do we now need government permission to have private parties on our own property? Apparently so, according to these supervisors, it is considered marketing. "The Fauquier ordinance clearly violates Virginia's Right to Farm Act, which guarantees agriculture activities of growing and selling." (Mark J. Fitzgibbons, The Washington Examiner, August 12, 2012)

I heard Martha speak to a gathering of 25 friends, farmers, and vintners from Fauquier County. She brought a basket laden with tomatoes and peppers grown on her Liberty Farm, vegetables that she is no longer allowed to sell. She can give them away to food banks. Through passionate tears, she outlined her childhood dream of owning a farm, finding the perfect land in 2006, and the six year nightmare that followed.

Martha's 70 acre farm is located in Fauquier County, a rural, agricultural community 15 minutes from Washington, D.C. if the traffic cooperates. The rich soil in the area is perfect for growing grapes and producing wine. Many of the rich farm landowners understand farming as running beautiful horses and leaving the land unspoiled – actual farming is a nuisance and an inconvenience. They are the "penny loafer farmers," as someone had named them. They are offended by Martha's farm that actually produces food that people need and enjoy.

Martha bought her farm with an agricultural conservation easement. Since there was no mention of any activities that she could not engage in on her farm, she proceeded to repair the historical barn. She built an apiary, harvested hay, grew herbs, and rescued 165 animals, sold chicken, duck, turkey, emu eggs, candles made from beeswax, birdhouses, and fiber from lamas and alpacas. She had a business license. A lot of hard work went into breathing life into the previously abandoned piece of property. The grass was five feet high and the barn was leaning when she bought the property.

She was told through letters and unauthorized inspections on her property that she could not even cut grass on her property. She had to fence off 20 acres for 2 years because it was considered "hallowed ground" although nobody has ever died there during the Civil War; it had been just an encampment area. Animals and children could not seek shelter from heat or play under a beautiful oak grove. The family was never reimbursed for the fencing or the loss of use of their property for two years – it was a "clerical error."

A trench was dug to prevent parking on her property because it obscured the view shed. Although holding a business permit and special permit to operate a farm store, her business permit has recently not been renewed by the county. Liberty Farm is the only farm in focus for this environmental harassment. What happened to property rights and economic freedom in our country?

Some Americans are waking up to the insidious UN Agenda 21 across the country. Their legal battles come in many forms at the local and state levels, all involving zoning issues, driven by one ultimate goal, global governance.

UN Agenda 21 "soft law" document has been in place and ratified in Rio, Brazil, by 178 countries since 1992. The recommendations that are not legally binding but morally obligatory provide specific rules about local organizations and their practices, limiting everyone's behavior and freedom.

The idea of global governance, a.k.a. UN Agenda 21, was seeded a hundred years ago. Americans and their private property are under such a concerted and well-orchestrated attack, that it has become a full assault on private property and redistribution of wealth in the last stages of full implementation.

Would ordinary Americans succeed in deflecting and destroying the evil UN Agenda 21, the multi-headed Hydra? It is a hard question to answer since a good majority of Americans are blissfully unaware of what is going on under their noses nor do they seem to care.

The privileged elites are so convinced they are best suited to rule the world, that they are willing to dedicate their vast fortunes to achieve global governance. Cecil Rhodes, for example, of the Rhodes scholarship, believed that the whole world should be dominated by the British Empire. His vision is no longer a possibility since the once mighty British Empire is now overrun by hostile Muslims thanks to its failed and misguided multi-culturalism.

The modern granddaddy of globalism is Maurice Strong. "Since Cecil Rhoades, ...there has been a group of people who actually believe that society is best served when it is managed by a benevolent government populated by the enlightened intelligentsia." Many Congressmen on both sides of the aisle support globalism, thus Agenda 21. The International Monetary Fund (IMF) published a report in April 2010, detailing the creation of a global currency as the path to global economic stability. (Henry Lamb, Founding Director of Freedom21, Inc.)

The main stream media does not discuss Agenda 21 and has labeled those that do tin foil hat conspiracy theorists. Americans believe what they are told by the MSM until they have problems keeping their farms, use their land, build a fence, plant a tree, a bush, use rainwater on their property, build a barn, plant a garden, or use trees to shade animals. Once property owners run afoul of the many permits they are required to get, they become believers.

There is no end to the asinine rules that various Boards of Supervisors write and implement. These boards are populated by individuals who pretend to be Republicans in order to get elected but are Democrats who enjoy controlling the sheeple minions in their counties.

Liberals love to micro-manage other people's lives. If you are unlucky and belong to a Home Owner's Association, you will witness first-hand the self-appointed tyrannical behavior of little people with power to turn your existence upside down on your own land.

The control does not stop there. On August 21, 2012, Dick Morris TV discussed "Obama's War on Suburbs" - how "Obama wants suburban taxes to fund inner city projects and he applies UN Agenda 21 to force people to move to the cities. ...Barack Obama opposes suburbs. He wants to force everyone into the cities from whence our ancestors fled. He wants the suburban revenue to subsidize the inner cities. ...Because of carbon emissions and global warming, we have to reduce the dependence on the automobile, increase people walking and biking and we have to reshape the way we live with that in mind."

The environmentalist concern over carbon emissions and Obama's funneling resources to the inner cities from the suburbs combine into Obama's program called regionalism. He has already given regionalism planning grants in Ohio, Virginia, and Florida. Regionalism means getting rid of counties, cities, suburban government and put everything under the regional authority. The regional entity governs and makes all decisions for a large metropolitan area such as transportation, zoning, land use, education, wetlands, funding, open space regulations, and environmental regulations, all designed to force people from the suburbs into the cities. (dickmorris.com/obamas-war-on-suburbs-dick-morris-tv-lunch-alert/)

Unnecessary traffic jams and congestion on suburban roads, taking access roads out of circulation, blocking zones and roads to traffic, narrowing roads, high and frequent speed bumps, arcane and expensive regulations, expensive gas, road fines, drones hovering over our homes, expensive tolls for roads, are designed to force people to move back into the cities. President Obama wants to fundamentally change the way we live.

Global governance restricts individual freedom by setting up rigid environmental rules and regulations that set limits on individual behavior, on organizations, and on businesses, covering every facet of human life. Non-elected bureaucrats and NGOs (non-governmental organizations) set policy and decide what is good for a community through "visioning" committees and grants.

"Visioning" grants come from the EPA and other federal agencies to local communities slated to undergo the visioning or zoning change and to the American Planning Association that would help states develop model legislation favoring their re-zoning plans and re-distribution of property and wealth.

Local planning agencies, an NGO, or ICLEI (International Council for Local Environmental Initiatives) start the process of sustainable development, sustainable community, or green growth and request a federal grant. Who is going to oppose the "greening" of their area and protecting the environment for their children's future? It is land use control plain and simple by the local, state, or federal government bureaucrats.

Control of land use denies "farmers the right to sell their land to city dwellers because of an urban boundary zone, or greenbelt, or conservation area, or because of the 'unjust compensation tax.'" Worse yet, farmers themselves are not allowed to use their own land and are fenced in, forbidden to use it or develop it at all. Water can be denied or cut off to an entire village or town. The installation of septic tanks is forbidden in Maryland, discouraging farmers to build on their own property. The conduits of such restrictions of the behavior of land owners and farmers are the Board of Supervisors through re-zoning and permit.

Martha's plight is one example of thousands across the country who are fighting their local zoning czars for economic freedom, the use of their land, property rights, free of intrusive, photographed, unauthorized, and illegal, often in the middle of the night land and home inspections, and the freedom to engage in encumbered agricultural activities from environmental groups funded by wealthy globalists who would rather see humans disappeared or moved into government approved urban ghettoes where they can be better controlled and herded. Fortunately for Martha and for Virginians, on July 1, 2014, HB268 became law, giving small farmers protection from overburdening regulations and fees by local governments, and freedom to sell the fruits, vegetables, eggs, dairy, honey, wool, and other farm-produced goods.

White House Council on Strong Cities, Strong Communities

A new Executive Order issued on March 15, 2012, established a White House Council on Strong Cities, Strong Communities.(SC2)

The Executive Order formed another bureaucracy to "lift communities out of distress," and to "support comprehensive planning and regional collaboration." Communities would not be in distress if the economy and the country were not purposefully destroyed through burdensome regulations, insane energy policy, directives, wasteful stimuli, resolutions, omnibus overspending bills, and executive orders.

The Council is a "pilot initiative" that partners with "cities and regions to augment their vision of stability and economic growth." This partnership aims to drive communities toward "regional planning" that leads to "sustained economic growth."

The end goal of the initiative is to persuade regions to accept federal resources more effectively and efficiently to develop and implement economic strategies to "become more competitive, sustainable, and inclusive." There will be strings attached to these federal resources. The operating words are "sustainable," and "regional" or "regionalism," buzzwords for UN Agenda 21.

The Council on Strong Cities, Strong Communities will operate within the Department of Housing and Urban Development, chaired by the Secretary of HUD and the Assistant to the President for Domestic Policy.

The mission and function of the Council will be to develop and implement various components of **Strong Cities, Strong Communities**, or in bureaucratic code, *SC2*, as determined by Co-Chairs: economic vision, strategies, and technical assistance to local governments.

The Council on Strong Cities, Strong Communities must incorporate their efforts into the agency's annual performance plans and the outcomes of annual performance results. Economic growth and local capacity of cities and local governments must be addressed.

The federal government will assist communities in "building local capacity to address economic issues, comprehensive planning, and advancing regional collaboration."

The Council shall conduct "outreach to representatives of nonprofit organizations, businesses, labor organizations, State and local government agencies, school districts, elected officials, faith and other community based organizations, philanthropies, other institutions of local importance, and other interested persons with relevant expertise in the expansion and improvement of efforts to build local capacity to address economic issues in cities and communities."

Annual meetings will be conducted with mayors and city employees to share "findings and progress, offer best practices, and promote strategies that have worked in communities participating in the initiative."

Yearly reports will be required to "demonstrate more efficient and effective use of federal resources." It is not clear what the federal resources will be, however, since so many departments are part of the Council on Strong Cities, Strong Communities (SC2), it appears to be a massive expansion of federal government involvement into the operation of the states and local governments. Key operating words throughout the Executive Order are economic local capacity and regional collaboration.

I focused immediately on the phrase, "regional collaboration," because it points to another tentacle of the UN Agenda 21 octopus. I recognized the language of HB 430 in Virginia, which established a "Regional Cooperation Incentive Fund," to offer an increased amount of government grant money to planning commissions that consolidate or coordinate with other local planners, thus regionalize.

What is wrong with regionalization? It is a step toward globalization. It is another layer of unaccountable, unelectable, and parasitic government. Municipalities are shaped into borderless groups that develop comprehensive plans in many areas but especially land use. These plans supersede local laws and often disregard property rights. The unelected layer of "regional" government will then ask each community to bring their laws and zoning in line with those of the "region."

Legislators should not use state tax money to implement regional comprehensive plans. Planning belongs at the local level by their elected officials. This new Executive Order forces regionalization in every state through initiatives, schemes, and visions, attached to federal grants in order to bribe citizens to "regionalize," a step closer to total federal control of every aspect of our daily lives.

Epilogue

When President Obama says, "We don't need more roads in the suburbs," he is pushing and forcing us into the United Nations Agenda 21. On my recent trip to Europe, I experienced the many effects of Agenda 21 compliance.

A small wind turbine was slowly turning next to a gas station in a field in Romania. Nearby was a small well, pumping crude oil.

Lighting was so poor everywhere, I could hardly see to put make-up on in the morning. Anemic, low wattage CFL bulbs cast a dim glow that made me feel sick.

Smart meters had turned off the AC in the lobby of the four star hotel where I stayed. The wide-open doors did not help reduce the stifling hot atmosphere. Rooms were allowed AC with the door key. Fancy bathroom mirrors in the lobby had tiny television sets imbedded in the middle. I would have preferred air conditioning.

Decrepit multi-storied apartments had banks of brand new and shiny smart meters in the lobby. Cell towers were placed on rooftops of high-rise tenements approved by regional authorities.

Electricity use was drastically cut. The high price per kilowatt hour discouraged the use of appliances that we take for granted, placing them out of the reach of many consumers who lived on fixed incomes. Using a drier, if a person owned one, at the same time as a microwave oven, short-circuited the entire building.

Crops were scarce because many fertile fields were used for hundreds of windmills instead of producing grains and food.

Diesel was $10 a gallon and a new breed of bio fuel Diesel was almost $11 a gallon. This new Diesel Maxx contained a mixture of rapeseed oil, a vegetable plant that makes thick oil we used for cooking during the communist regime when foodstuff was in short supply.

Nobody was running air conditioning although it was 92 degrees Fahrenheit and very humid for early October. Europeans have been falsely conditioned by doctors and environmentalists that it is bad for one's health to use air conditioning and to drink anything chilled or with ice. Asking for ice cubes in Europe is perceived as nothing short of madness. European waiters roll their eyes and return with two ice cubes floating in a large glass of lukewarm beverage.

The airliner I chose to travel to Europe was KLM. Ever so environmentally conscious, KLM asked passengers to defray their carbon foot print of the flight by donating money to an environmental cause pushing Agenda 21 goals.

In order to change my ticket for another day, which normally would cost $150 in the United States, KLM charged me $674, the cost of almost another ticket. Most of the quoted price consisted of global and environmental taxes, including the transatlantic air tax which so far American airliners have refused to pay.

Wherever I went, lights were so dim that everything looked dingy and depressing. If you did not stumble in the dark stores and restaurants, you most certainly succumbed to cigarette smoke inhalation.

President Obama is going to make good on his promise to spread the wealth around through his global tax plan, the UN global governance, a plan to steal from the United States and distribute our wealth to third world nations that are really the backbone and the reason for the United Nation's existence. United Nations is no longer the peacekeeper it was intended to be and it does not represent the interests of the United States.

President Obama's second term will be dedicated to the agenda of man-made climate change, to amnesty for illegal aliens, and to the focused de-development of the United States with the help of the United Nations via global taxes and global governance. Here are some examples of such wealth-redistributive taxes that might be successfully levied in the U.S.:

- Billionaires Taxes (There are currently 1,600 billionaires across the globe, 400 in the U.S. alone.)
  How far of a stretch would it be to tax millionaires and then ordinary citizens when the revenue collected from billionaires is not enough?
- The Robin Hood Tax (The financial transaction tax involving every purchase of currency, stocks, bonds, real estate, or any transaction involving purchase of assets)
- Global cigarette tax
- Transatlantic air tax, a tax meant to offset the carbon emissions of airplanes flying to and from Europe (This is the very expensive tax I paid to fly with KLM, a Dutch carrier.)
  This tax is required by the European Union and is in excess of airport fees and taxes.
- The Law of the Sea Treaty gives the United Nations the right to tax nations for the right to explore minerals and oil on the sea bed, fish, and move in global waters. The taxes charged will be paid to the "Authority" which in turn will distribute the proceeds to the United Nations. After paying itself the lion's share, UN will distribute the rest to third world nations, particularly land-locked countries. A percentage of royalties from underwater oil wells will also be distributed to third world nations. An additional tax associated with LOST is the carbon tax levied because of the marine thermal pollution presumably caused by the United States.

All these taxes are part of the master plan for global redistribution of wealth from the United States to the third world via the stewardship of the United Nations under the umbrella of global governance. The global transfer of taxes is not going to help poor people in third world nations. The money will go to the corrupt dictators who run these nations and dominate the discussion and policy at the United Nations. All the foreign aid that we give third world nations is never used for good – it buys weapons to further the wars between factions that are fighting for control and dominance. Those in power take the foreign aid that becomes the means to succeed in their plans to control the population and keep it poor, undermining free enterprise and economic freedom.

According to Dick Morris, President Obama plans to sign various treaties in the lame duck session of Congress that would obligate the United States "in perpetuity" to fund dictatorships and causes that are contrary to American values until "the Senate rejects it or the new President renounces it." Under the Vienna Convention, the President's signature suffices and ratification by Congress is not necessary. (Dick Morris TV: Lunch Alert, October 8, 2012)

A treaty to regulate the Internet will be signed in December 2012 in Dubai. Although the proceedings are held in secret, we do know that the United Nations will control and Internet, assigning IP addresses to people, requiring them to notify the host country of their IP address. United Nations will censor who uses Internet and will charge excessive fees to those individuals accessing websites outside of their countries, a form of taxation. We invented the Internet. Must we now relinquish it to the power and control of the United Nations?

Hillary Clinton is going to sign a global code of conduct which will put United States in the position of being unable to defend itself or start a war without the approval of the Security Council, more specifically, Russia and China.

Although defeated in July 2012, the Small Arms Treaty might still be signed during the lame duck session of Congress, putting Americans in the position of having to give up their hunting and self-defense weapons. (Dick Morris and Eileen McGann, *Here Come the Black Helicopters!*)

Is this the kind of country we want to live in? Do we want to give up our wealth, weapons, the ability to defend ourselves, our economic freedom, our property, our country, our way of life, and sovereignty to the United Nations, run by tin pot third world dictators, in the name of "social justice" dictated by Agenda 21?

ABOUT THE AUTHOR

A former Economics college Adjunct Professor with thirty years teaching experience, the author grew up in communist Romania during the brutal regime of Nicolae Ceausescu. She has the unique perspective of a totalitarian regime and values freedom and the opportunity for success that natural born Americans take for granted. She warns of the daily loss of freedoms that are threatening our sovereignty as the United Nations is attempting to dismantle America piece by piece, turning it into its "global" fiefdom.

A weekly segment radio commentator for Butler on Business, Liberty Express Radio, Silvio Canto Jr. Blog Talk Radio, and senior columnist for Canada Free Press, as well as usactionnews.com, the author uses her extensive knowledge to inform thousands of readers and listeners. Because she speaks several languages and has taught four during her college career, Dr. Johnson Paugh can read the news as they happen around the globe.

Her previous books, "Echoes of Communism," and "Liberty on Life Support" are available at Amazon in paperback and Kindle.

"Echoes of Communism" is a compilation of childhood experiences, describing the daily life in a totalitarian state: religion, superstitions, poverty, confiscation of property, social engineering, education, and lack of freedom of speech. She describes the harsh reality of communist life, not the romanticized version taught in American public schools and promoted by the main stream media. A sequel to "Echoes of Communism" is currently in the works.

"Liberty on Life Support" presents essays on American exceptionalism, education, the U.S. economy, and immigration, reflecting the massive destructive changes that took place in our country in the past eight years.

The author can be reached through her website, ileanajohnson.com, her Facebook author page, and her blog, romanianconservative.blogspot.com.